dreams

by Tucker Shaw

AlloyBooks

To Mother T., the world's best dreamer.

ACKNOWLEDGMENTS: Mad, mad thanks to every dreamy person who helped me out. Especially Susan Kaplow for the opportunity. Representing Alloy: Angie Maximo, Fiona Gibb, Lauren Goodman, Deb Goldstein. Representing 17th St. Productions: Les Morgenstein, Ann Brashares, Josh Bank, Cecily von Ziegesar, Jodi Anderson, Russell Gordon, Lauren Monchik, and Marc Stüwe. And much love to the captains of this dream team: Matt Diamond, Jim Johnson, and Sam Gradess. Most of all, thanks to everyone in the Alloy.com community who generously shared their dreams with me. Y'all need some serious help.

ALLOYBOOKS
Published by the Penguin Group
Penguin Putnam Books for Young Readers,
345 Hudson Street, New York, New York 10014, U.S.A.
Penguin Books Ltd, 27 Wrights Lane, London W8 5TZ, England
Penguin Books Australia Ltd, Ringwood, Victoria, Australia
Penguin Books Canada Ltd, 10 Alcorn Avenue, Toronto, Ontario, Canada M4V 3B2
Penguin Books (N.Z.) Ltd, 182-190 Wairau Road, Auckland 10, New Zealand

Penguin Books Ltd, Registered Offices: Harmondsworth, Middlesex, England

Published by Puffin Books,
a division of Penguin Putnam Books for Young Readers, 2000

10 9 8 7 6 5 4 3 2 1

Produced by 17th Street Productions,
an Alloy Online, Inc. company
33 West 17th Street
New York, NY 10011

introduction

so the other day

I'm sitting there at some random coffee shop, minding my own business, and my good friend Adam comes walking by.

"Hey!" he goes.

"Hey, what's up," I go.

"What's new? How's things?"

I had to think for a moment. See, I'd been working on this book—the very one you're holding in your hands—and I was struggling with some part of it (I can't remember which part). "Pretty good," I said. "Just working on a book about dreams."

"Ugh," goes Adam. "I can't stand all that stuff. I think it's such a waste of time. Who cares if you understand your dreams? I wake up, and that's it. Useless."

Man, thanks a lot, I was thinking. Don't count on a free copy. And while you're at it, get outta my face. "Have a nice day," I said.

But he got my brain running. Why do we care about dreams?

Some people say you can understand yourself better if you understand your dreams. Some people think you can solve problems by looking for answers in your dreams. Some people just get a kick out of them.

Me, I didn't really know. But I knew I couldn't get Adam's comment out of my head.

But that night I had a great dream, which cleared it all up. See, every now and then, when I've got a problem floating around my brain, Bootsy Collins shows up in my dreams. He's like my fairy godfather or something—he's always got the answers. That night he gave me a message (he didn't use words—he used his bass guitar, but I understood) and it went something like this: "Chill out, man. Relax. Have some fun. It's all good."

I woke up, and I knew. Dreams are fun. And analyzing them is fun. That's right, fun. And that's what this book is about.

Sure, I'll give you the lowdown on what dreams are, why they happen, and what some experts say about them. (Just think—you'll be able to impress your friends with big words like *somnambulism* and small words like *Jung*.) And I'll share some truly twisted dreams I've gotten from real people like yourself and help you understand what they mean. In fact, when you're done here, you'll be able to interpret your own dreams and other people's. (Hey, and if you get good enough at it, you can charge people. *Kaching!*)

But the bottom line? This book is for fun. Hope you have some.

The other thing Adam said to me was, "And besides, what do you know about dreams?" Now, there's a good question. I have no formal training. I've never been to a dream institute. I've never incubated a dream with ancient Egyptologists (although I used to watch Isis a lot when I was a kid). I don't have an advanced degree in dream theory. I'm not even sure you can get one. But ever since I was a kid, I've loved the trips I go on every single night. As a writer and columnist, I've analyzed hundreds of dreams, and they never get boring to me. I love reading about dreams, talking about dreams. I can't wait to get to bed at night.

I hope this book makes your nightly trips a little more fun, too.

*Bootsy Collins is the grand master of all funksters.
Without him there'd be no Parliament-Funkadelic—
and then where would we be? No one's played a
funkier bass guitar ever, and no one ever will.*

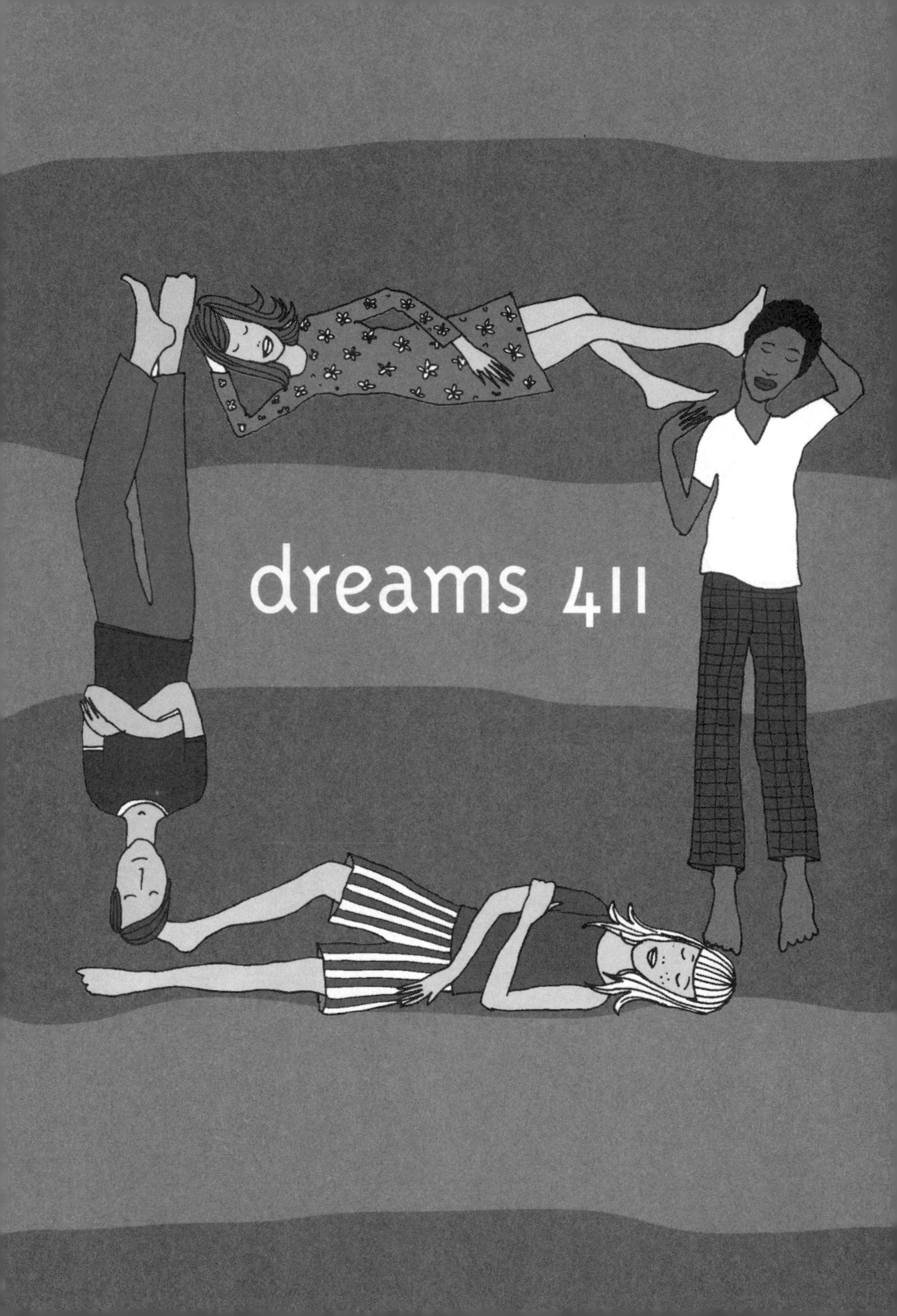
dreams 411

dreams defy science. We really
know very little about them. (We really know very little
about the whole, entire brain, but that's another story.)

Why are they so elusive? Because they don't fit into
the "real" world. They're just too weird.

But there are some things we do know. We know
that everyone dreams. We know that everyone dreams
every single night. We know that if we look at them
closely enough, dreams can be very revealing. We
know a bit about what's going on in your brain and
body when you dream. We know about how different
cultures think about dreams. We know that dreams are
crazy, colorful, exciting, really strange, and sometimes
scary as hell.

Read on, and I'll break it all down for you.

Everyone Dreams

Everyone dreams. Get it? Everyone. It's a biological fact.

But not everyone remembers their dreams. Why? Who knows. Maybe some people have too much on their minds. Maybe their dreams are too boring to remember. Maybe they're too disturbing to remember. Maybe some people just don't think dreams are worth remembering.

People like that are missing out. Most dreams are way too fun and trippy to blow off.

The problem? Well, our brains edit stuff—conscious and unconscious stuff—in ways that we really don't understand. Even those of us who pay attention to our dreams don't remember all of them. It's just not totally within our control.

Luckily there are ways to get better at remembering your dreams. See? Over to the side there. Five handy-dandy tips. Oh, and there's way more useful information in the "Do It Yourself" section (see page 99).

⋆ *Alloy User Poll* ⋆

HOW OFTEN DO YOU REMEMBER YOUR DREAMS?

26% Every night!
73% Sometimes but not always
1% Never

Dream no small dreams for

Tips to Better Remember Your Dreams

1 You gotta really want to. Every dream book out there will tell you that the most important thing in remembering your dreams is that you have to want to. Before you fall asleep, you should say to yourself, three times, "Hey! Remember a dream tonight, all right? Jeez!" Sounds whacked, I know, but it's worth a shot.

2 Start writing down and talking about your dreams. Ask other people about theirs. Write about dreams for your creative-writing class. Try hard, every morning while you're brushing your teeth, to remember a dream from last night. Check out dream sites on-line. The more you think about dreams, the more you'll remember them.

3 See page 122, "Dream Catching."

4 Try the bladder technique. You're more likely to remember dreams if you wake up suddenly. One way to do it? Drink an extra glass or two of water before bed. You'll definitely get up in the middle of the night to pee. Keep a pencil and paper in the bathroom so you can write down your dreams.

5 Take a nap sitting up. When your head bobs over and you wake up, see if you can remember what you were dreaming. Most likely it won't be a big, involved thing because you won't have been asleep that long, but chances are you'll be able to remember an image, or a feeling, or something. Salvador Dalí, the wackiest painter ever, did this for inspiration.

they have the power to move the hearts of men. —Goethe

Your Dreams Are Yours and Yours Alone

Everything in your dreams comes from your brain. Everything.

Your dreams are like little movies that you create each night—you come up with the settings, characters, action, and ideas in your dreams all by yourself. See how creative you can be? You li'l Spielberg, you.

All the people and things in your dreams are there because you put them there. Obviously you didn't sit down and write it all out before you fell asleep, but your unconscious brain (my what?? see page 14 for details) created the whole thing from scratch. Why? Maybe for fun. Maybe to send you a message. Maybe to help you sort something out. Maybe to let you experience things you'd never be able to experience in real life. Every dream is different that way.

But one thing is for sure—everything and everyone in your dreams is a part of you. You heard it. Everything. And this is the key to dream analysis.

That house you're wandering through? Most likely it's a part of you that you're exploring. That freak who's chasing you? Part of you that's looking for some attention. Madonna? Maybe she represents a splashy part of you. A sinking ship? A part of yourself that might be going through a tough time. The crocodile you're sautéing? Part of you that you're ready to devour.

This isn't to say that people and things in your dreams

don't sometimes represent things in the world outside your head. But they represent what those people or things mean to you, what they symbolize, and how you feel about them. The fact that they are there, the way in which they are there, is all about you.

Get the picture? You created everything in your dream, and everything in your dream is a part of you. Period. This is one thing that every shrink, scientist, and dream analyst can agree on.

Round the World in a Dream

People all around the world have been dreaming since time began. Mostly people thought they were omens, or warnings, or something even trippier. Check it out:

GREECE

In among all those ancient Greek gods, there was Aesculapius, an important health and healing god who was believed to send medical advice and cures to people in their dreams. Greeks would journey to one of the hundreds of temples dedicated to him, where they would fast, perform a bunch of rituals, and sleep on the temple floor, hoping that Aesculapius would show up overnight and offer up some advice. The Greeks wrote volumes about dreams, including the oldest surviving dream dictionary, *Oneirocritica* (*The Interpretation of Dreams*), by Artemidorus. Yes, you can get your own copy at the bookstore. Warning: It isn't easy reading.

EGYPT

In ancient Egypt, dreams were thought to be messages from the gods. As a result, dreams meant big business. Professional dream interpreters set up temples all along the Nile to help people understand their dreams and to help people ask the gods to send answers to them in their sleep. There was even a god (Bes, sort of a dwarf who tells jokes)

The waking have one world in common; sleepers have

in charge of protecting people from nightmares, among other things. Much was written about dreams in ancient Egypt and Mesopotamia (in what is now Iraq), but very little survives.

INDIA

More than people of any other culture or religion, South Asian Hindus developed the idea that this world is actually a dream and "real" reality is somewhere else. The Vedas, the oldest Hindu scriptures (between three and four thousand years old), suggest that people are reincarnated back into this world, this dream, and it's only after breaking the cycle of reincarnation, or "waking up" from this dream world, that they'll understand the truth and become complete.

CHINA

Traditional Chinese philosophy, developed over the past five thousand years, says that while you're sleeping, your spirit (which looks exactly like you) leaves your body for nighttime adventures. Voilà! Dreams! The sucky part happens when you wake up before your soul gets back to your body—you get all groggy and irritable until it makes its way back. This point of view says alarm clocks are violent and unhealthy. (Right on!) The Chinese were also ahead of the game in believing that a dream has a lot to do with the dreamer—they'd take into account your astrology, your living situation, and your age when interpreting your dream.

each a private world of his own.—Heraclitus, Fragments

THE AMERICAS

Before Columbus came along, North and South America were made up of thousands of distinct cultures, languages, and beliefs, but one thing almost every group paid attention to was dreams. Dreams were seen as important for creative inspiration, spiritual guidance, and even forecasting weather and hunting conditions. Some groups, like the Raramuri in northern Mexico, arranged their sleeping patterns so they would wake during the night to discuss their dreams with one another.

AFRICA

African cultures, some of the oldest on the planet, were all over the place when it came to dreams—not so surprising when you consider the hugeness of the continent and the diversity of its people. They ran the gamut and still do: some believed that dreams are as important as waking experiences and others discouraged dreaming and talking about dreaming altogether. One West African group, the Ashanti, took dreams so much to heart, they would allow a husband to take legal action against another man if that man had an erotic dream about his wife.

Dreams and Religion

Christianity, Islam, and Judaism all have references to dreams in their scriptures. For example, after Jesus died, Saint Paul reported many dreams in which Jesus sent him messages of encouragement. Mohammed had a dream in which Gabriel transported him from Mecca to Jerusalem, where he chatted with Abraham, Moses, and Jesus. The Old Testament tells the story of Joseph (of the amazing multicolored dream coat—not to be confused with any coat of Donny Osmond's), who was an important dream interpreter. He is said to have saved Egypt from seven years of famine by interpreting the dreams of the pharaoh and advising him on what to do. His reward? Pharaoh made Joseph prime minister of Egypt. Nice gig.

THAT WE COME TO THIS EARTH TO LIVE IS UNTRUE:
WE COME BUT TO SLEEP, TO DREAM.
—TRADITIONAL AZTEC POEM

Shrinks & Dreams

Back in the old days, dreams were understood in three ways. They predicted the future, they were planted by a spirit or demon, or they were some sort of revelation or religious vision. Or all three.

But that changed around about the turn of last century. People started to see that dreams come straight outta the brain of the person dreaming. As in, dreams come from the inside, not the outside. Doesn't sound so shocking now, but at the beginning of the twentieth century this was major.

DR. FREUD

Around 1900 Dr. Sigmund Freud, already a very fashionable psychoanalyst in Austria (he worked mostly with chic, rich Europeans), published a book called *The Interpretation of Dreams* (not to be confused with the ancient Greek *Oneirocritica,* which also translates to "interpretation of dreams"). In it he outlined his ideas of consciousness and unconsciousness (check out that sidebar over on page 14) and proclaimed that all dreams were products of the unconscious mind.

The main reason people were so interested in Freud's picture of the unconscious was, well . . . sex. See, Freud estimated that around 90 percent of your mind falls under the category

Dr. Freud

Reason guides but a small part of man . . . the rest obeys

of unconsciousness, and he saw the unconscious as this wacky place jammed with deep, dark urges and desires, most of them sexual. He believed that we go through life beating down these violent urges, so they crop up in our dreams. Dreams, he believed, all came from the unconscious mind and are therefore always aggressive or sexual in nature—even if they need extensive "decoding" to get to the point. Through dreams we can live out these urges without them getting in the way of our real lives.

In other words, because the unconscious mind is, well, unconscious, it can't express itself the way we do in our daily lives. Therefore, needing to have a voice of its own, it takes over our dreams.

So if the unconscious is all about sex and violence, why aren't all dreams just straight-up sex and violence dreams? Freud would say that your unconscious mind understands that your conscious mind would freak out if all your dreams were like that, so it puts these dreams into code. Phallic symbols and stuff. You, then, get to decipher them—if you want to. (For a list of some common phallic symbols, check out pages 20 and 21.)

This was, and still is, a shocking and popular idea. *The Interpretation of Dreams* has sold zillions of copies all over the world and been translated into dozens of languages. Why? Well, his theory works in many ways because you really can make any dream fit into it. And since so many dreams are sexual or dark, anyway, it's not such a stretch to believe that maybe all dreams share that common thread. Plus, sex sells.

feeling, true or false, passion, good or bad.—Joseph Roux

DR. JUNG

Carl Jung was a Swiss psychoanalyst working around the same time as Freud. They even studied together for a few years. Many people claim that Jung learned everything he knew from Freud, but the fact is, Jung had his own thing going on way before he met Freud. And once Jung started to believe that Freud's point of view was too limited, he bolted. Then there was all this name-calling and stuff. Hello, soap opera.

Dr. Jung

Anyway, according to Jung, dreams aren't all about acting out impulses and urges. Dreams are more like windows into our unconscious that help us see and understand what we're about. Dreams help us get our lives—both conscious and unconscious—into balance.

For the record, Jung saw the unconscious as wicked complex, but less scary and violent than Freud did. Jung also broke down the unconscious into a couple of parts. One, the personal unconscious, is all yours. It's as unique as you are.

The other, called the collective unconscious, is one you share with the rest of the world. It's made up of really basic concepts that we all understand and deal with—concepts like "growing up" and "dealing with your family" and "defining yourself as an individual" and "having sex."

Jung made a connection between these concepts and certain characters and situations that we're all familiar with, which he called "archetypes" (see that list of 'em starting on page 16). Jung said that not only do these archetypes show up in everyone's dreams, but they show up in myths from every single culture on the planet. He also believed that this collective unconscious is innate, meaning all humans are born with it.

Yep, plenty of smart people have put a lot of effort into figuring out what dreams are and where they come from. But dreams are too personal, too bizarre, too unreal, and too, well, dreamy for anyone to completely nail them down. And probably no one will. That's why they're so cool.

Plenty more dream research and analysis has happened since the two big guys turned things around in the early twentieth century. Fritz Perls, an American therapist in the 1930s and 1940s, elaborated on the notion that dreams turn the dreamer into a character or an object to tell a story. Medard Boss, a Swiss psychologist in the 1940s and 1950s, said it was a waste of time to find deeper meaning in dreams, that the meaning is right there on the surface if you choose to see it. And Patricia Garfield, a contemporary American dream expert, trains people to control their dreams and use them to confront issues they're facing in real life. (Want to conjure up a specific dream for yourself? See page 40, "Famous Dreamers.")

people chasing me from town to town.—Belle and Sebastian

Conscious? Unconscious? Huh?

★ Your unconscious and conscious are both part of the same thing—your brain. The thing is, your conscious mind is accessible, but your unconscious isn't. Your conscious mind usually makes sense to you, but your unconscious mind does things and feels things in ways that aren't logical. For example, you may break curfew consciously to hang out with friends, but unconsciously you're testing the boundaries between you and your parents. Get it?

★ Freud and Jung argued about this back in their day, but since then, plenty of other experts have come up with new ideas. Compared to Freud, most experts put forth pretty mellow versions of the unconscious— less sex-and-violence driven. Some see consciousness as a sliding scale, from "full" conscious, where you're focused on something and thinking about it (like homework), to "semi" conscious, where you're doing something but not really thinking about it (like chewing gum and letting your mind wander), and so on, right on down to unconscious (sleeping).

★ Some people believe the unconscious is your soul. Some see it as your spirit. Some think it lasts after you die. Some see it as totally nonexistent, something we make up with our conscious minds to explain things we don't understand.

★ The bottom line is that no one really understands this on a scientific level because it just isn't scientific. It doesn't exist on a physical level, so it's impossible to measure or analyze. All we can do is guess.

I think dreaming is our way of

Some of Jung's Major Archetypes

Jung believed that everyone on the planet, regardless of culture, age, or location, shares certain dream images that have common, deeper meanings. That's why these images show up in so many stories and myths around the world. And Jung believed that these images, in one form or another, are in everyone's dreams, too.

THE MOTHER

The mother is the source of life, the thing that brought you here. This archetype often takes the shape of the earth, or food, or a womb, or a house, or a female figure. Often it's a warm, safe, encompassing image, but sometimes it's evil and threatening.

THE HERO

You know, the dashing guy or girl who saves the day. Not usually someone with special powers, the hero is just a regular person who does a good thing. Often in your dreams the hero is you.

THE TRICKSTER OR PRANKSTER

Not necessarily a "bad" person or spirit but someone who causes trouble and mocks human beings along the way. In your dreams this comes across as an obstacle.

MASCULINE AND FEMININE

Also called yin/yang or Adam and Eve, this archetype isn't really about a character; it's more about the relationship between opposites. Both sides need the other to

being psychic on a subconscious level.—‹‹Jessrit››

exist, but at the same time they're often at odds. Jung believed that each of us has both sides inside and that our dreams help us balance them.

THE DIVINE CHILD

Jesus is the most famous divine child but not the only one. In our dreams, situations of newness, change, or growth are often represented by a variation of the divine child. It's generally a hopeful image. (Note: It doesn't have to be a child. It could be a new flower or a new PlayStation game.)

THE SHADOW

It's like the anti-you. The shadow is everything that you shun or don't like about yourself, or don't want to know about yourself, or are afraid of in yourself. In your dreams this shadow could be anything from a monster, to a storm, to, well, a mirror image of yourself.

THE WISE OLD MAN OR WOMAN

This image includes magicians, wizards, priests, healers or doctors, teachers, and other authority figures. In your dreams, just because they appear wise doesn't always mean they give out the best advice.

It is easier to go to Mars or to the Moon than it is to

penetrate one's own being.—C. G. Jung

Sex & Dreams

Dream 1: You're making out with the movie star of your dreams, and you feel his or her hands crawling underneath your shirt. Is it about sex? Yup.

Dream 2: You're sitting on the top of a train, right up front. The train keeps going in and out of a tunnel. In and out. In and out. Is it about sex? Maybe. But it could be about frustration. Or control. Or fear of the dark. Or all kinds of stuff I can't even think of.

There are people (like Freud) who believe that every dream you have, every impulse you feel, every wish you wish, has something, something deep, to do with sex. Sound crazy? Maybe. But if those people aren't completely right, they're at least partially right.

We all (yes, including you and me) think about sex a lot. Even when we don't want or mean to. (Sex!) The topic just pops up (sex!) in our minds every now and then. (Sex!) It doesn't mean we have dirty minds (sex!); it just means we're human. Shouldn't be surprising, then (sex!), that sex also blasts its way into your dreams all the time. (Sex!)

And since we're not allowed to talk about sex as much as we think about sex, maybe, just maybe, we have to make up for it after hours. If you know what I mean. Which would make dreams even more sex-crazed than real life. Especially for some of us (not me, of course).

And if you think hard, you can interpret pretty much any dream as a sex dream. Including that dream about the stone leprechaun that came to life and danced around you.

We that are twain by day, at night are one. A dream can bring

(The awakening of a desire?) And the one about a cute li'l bunny eating an orange. (A forbidden fruit scenario, with the bunny representing your, uh, business?)

Okay, but seriously, you and I know that sex isn't the only thing we think about . . . or dream about. We dream about power, anxiety, comfort, sports, Double-Stuf Oreos (oh, wait . . . that might be about sex). It's easy enough to find sexual content in any dream you have, but then it's easy enough to find sexual content in any real-world experience, too. Doesn't mean that's what it's really about.

In the end, it's up to you what your dream is about. Sex? Okay! Something else? Okay! Your call.

Welcome to the 21st Century

*T*here's way more going on sexually in our daily lives than there was in Freud's heyday. Ads and TV and movies let us experience sexuality almost constantly. Is this a good thing? You decide. But it does mean we aren't quite as likely to conjure up twin volcanoes when we're really dreaming about boobs. We all know what they look like, so why not just conjure up boobs?

But sexuality was portrayed a lot less openly a hundred years ago. So it's certainly possible that before such major exposure to sex, people were more likely to subvert their sexual thoughts and make phallic symbols out of everyday items, especially in their dreams.

Which doesn't mean we don't still have dreams filled with symbols, phallic and otherwise. We do, but maybe not to the extent Freud imagined. Just like anyone else's, Freud's ideas were influenced by his time. After all, sometimes a cigar is just a cigar. Isn't it?

me to your arms once more.—Lizette Reese, from <u>Compensation</u>

Phallic Symbols

A phallic symbol is an image reminiscent of the sex organ (and therefore funny in that sixth-grade-health-class kind of way).

Though technically the term phallus means male sex organ, there are male and female phallic symbols. (We call the female ones phallic symbols because, well, no one's come up with a better word yet.) Some are more obvious than others. Snake = male, dough-nut = female. Below, a list of random items that could be phallic. Enjoy!

MALE

Banana

Necktie

Gun

Snake

Snowboard, surfboard, skateboard

Pencil

Train (especially one going through a tunnel)

Hot dog

Twinkies (or any other cream-filled snack cake)

Knife

Telephone pole

Key

Candlestick

Hammer

Beehive hairdo (à la Marge Simpson)

Ice cream cone, lollipop

Baseball bat, golf club

Trombone

Empire State Building

Electrical plug

Lightbulb

A person gets from a symbol

FEMALE

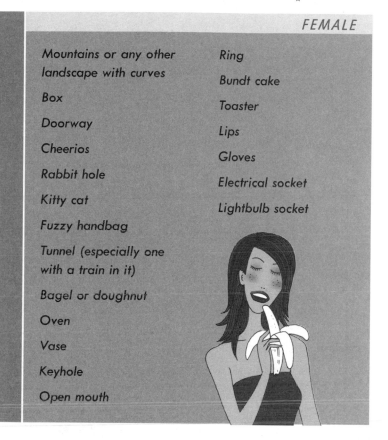

Mountains or any other landscape with curves

Box

Doorway

Cheerios

Rabbit hole

Kitty cat

Fuzzy handbag

Tunnel (especially one with a train in it)

Bagel or doughnut

Oven

Vase

Keyhole

Open mouth

Ring

Bundt cake

Toaster

Lips

Gloves

Electrical socket

Lightbulb socket

get this!

Not all sex dreams are even about sex. Lots of times your brain uses sex as a way of making a different point altogether. For example, if you find yourself doing it with, say, Will Smith, but in real life you don't even think he's all that, your dream could be about your own desire to be as successful as he is. You're connecting with his achievements, not his body.

the meaning he puts into it.—Justice Robert Jackson

Wet Dreams. They Aren't Just for Guys.

Okay, say you're a guy. It's morning. The alarm goes off and you're only half awake, so you don't think much about it until you hit the shower and realize that, dude, you're a little sticky.

Nice. You scored last night! High five!

Well, not really. You had a sex dream that ended with you ejaculating.

(Okay, say you're not a guy; you're a girl. You didn't ejaculate, but you can't help feeling, well, like something happened. After all, sex dreams are equal opportunity.)

What's it mean? Just like your conscious mind, your unconscious mind is, shall we say, a little horny. And sometimes it just has to take care of business. Self-shag.

Here's the thing: Wet dreams are totally normal. Even for girls. It's even normal never to have any at all. Everybody's different.

The first time I woke up all gooey (I think I was thirteen), I was terrified as hell, and I thought I was oozing alien blood

morning woodies

They say that guys of all ages have at least four erections a night. An erection upon waking is the remnant of one of these. These erections don't correspond with sex dreams necessarily—it's all about blood flowing around your body during the night.

or something. I had no idea what was going on—I didn't even remember having a dream. But later that day my friend Jay gave me the heads up on what had happened. And let me tell you, I couldn't wait to go back to sleep.

(I really hope my parents aren't reading this.)

Anyway, the first time I remember having a sex dream (which happened way later), I was even more freaked out. That's because it was the illest dream ever, involving a wide range of characters involved in an astonishing array of activities. I won't go into details. But I was convinced I was the original freak of nature.

Then I learned this: Just because you did it in your dream doesn't mean you'll do it in real life. It doesn't even mean you want to. What happens in dreams is unique and unusual and nobody else's business. (Aww, yeah!)

Having lots of sex dreams doesn't mean you're a perv. It means you're just like everyone else. And it's the safest sex going.

★ Alloy User Poll ★

HOW OFTEN
DO YOU DREAM
ABOUT SEX?

8% All the time!
74% Now and then
18% Never

Nightmares

Sometimes the dreams we remember best are the ones that scare us the most. You know, those incredibly detailed and vivid dreams that usually end up with you waking up, freaked out but relieved it's over. We've all had 'em—being chased, or falling off a cliff, or racing to save someone but being unable to move, or being asked out by President Clinton (my most horrifying nightmare of the past year), or whatever.

Kids up to the age of seven or so seem to have the worst nightmares, or at least they have the hardest time dealing with them because they're still working on the difference between reality and dreams. As far as kids are concerned, lying there in the dark, the monster they just dreamed about really is under the bed. It's not until they're a little older that they're able to say, "Okay, whew. Bad dream. Over."

Bad dreams get easier to deal with as we get older, but we're all hit with a really freaky one every now and then (see comment about President Clinton above). Sometimes you can link a really bad

To sleep, perchance to dream.

dream to being stressed out or having the flu, but you can have one any old time. In fact, some people believe we have at least one nightmare a night.

Luckily we don't remember them all. Unfortunately, the nightmares we do remember can be absolutely terrifying. Sucks, doesn't it?

Not really.

See, first of all, nightmares can't hurt you physically. Second of all, nightmares don't mean you're in danger in your real life.

Nightmares aren't "real" in any way. But like all dreams, especially the ones you remember vividly, they probably say something interesting and important about you, and you should pay attention. Analyze 'em.

Remember, it's your own brain that's coming up with this stuff. Not some mean guy down the street tormenting you. From setting, to plot, to characters, to everything— you wrote the script. And if you've cast yourself in the role of the person being chased or attacked or harmed or scared, you did it for a reason.

★ **Alloy User Poll** ★

WHEN WAS THE LAST TIME YOU HAD A NIGHTMARE?

54% Within the last month
18% Within the last year
28% I can't remember!

Maybe to justify nasty feelings you have about someone. Maybe to signify an important change. Maybe to test yourself. Maybe to "practice" for an upcoming challenge. Only you know. Think it over.

Ay, there's the rub.—Shakespeare, <u>Hamlet</u>

These are the most common nightmares I've come across. Drumroll, please . . .

1 FALLING! Some people think these dreams— which everyone has—are evolutionary throwbacks to our monkey and ape ancestors, who were constantly falling out of trees while sleeping. Falling dreams almost always end before you hit the ground, but if you do hit the ground, it doesn't mean anything bad.

2 BEING CHASED BY WILD ANIMALS AND MONSTERS! The thing chasing you probably represents someone or something you're pissed at in real life. It might be the actual person you're mad at (like that dream in which your math teacher mowed you down with his car) or not (like that dream where the alien trapped you in a half nelson—which, when you analyze it, turns out to be about your computer that keeps crashing).

3 BEING NAKED IN FRONT OF OTHER PEOPLE! Everyone has this dream. Sometimes it's about feeling unprepared. Sometimes it's about being afraid of revealing your "true" self. Sometimes it's not a nightmare at all (see page 22, "Wet Dreams").

4 FIRE! NATURAL DISASTER! Dreams about fires, earthquakes, floods, and stuff like that shout out your feelings of not being in control. As in, something way bigger and more powerful than you is screwing up your life. But sometimes these dreams are

Sometimes life seems like a dream, especially when I look down and

about renewal—as in, after the disaster you rebuild everything, making it all fresh and new.

5 TEETH FALLING OUT! When it's a nightmare, this is a straight-up dream about helplessness and anxiety. Teeth are an important symbol because they're so valuable to us—what with eating and looking good and all. Many animals (dogs, wolves, apes, tigers, and very likely we humans way back when) bare their teeth as a display of power and ferocity. Losing them in a dream symbolizes a loss of control and power.

For more about these nightmares and other popular dream themes, check out page 70.

Freaky Dreams: Prophetic and Recurring

PROPHETIC DREAMS

Can dreams predict the future?

It doesn't really seem possible, does it?

But many people swear they've had dreams that came true. Like that friend of mine who swore he dreamed that the Yankees won the World Series two years in a row way before it really happened. Or that girl who told me she dreamed her grandmother's death the day before it happened.

If you ask me, though, these don't really count. Yeah, they're very cool and kind of spooky, but are they really prophetic? Think about this: The guy who dreamed about the Yankees has been a fan of the team since he was a kid, and the team was having a pretty good season when he had the dream. It's not such a stretch to think that his dream was a coincidence. Same goes for the girl. Dreaming about the death of an old person isn't unusual at all—in fact, it happens all the time. See, consciously or unconsciously, we associate old people with an end to life, and not necessarily in a bad way. Sure, the timing of her dream was freaky, but again, I chalk it up to coincidence.

★ Alloy User Poll ★

EVER HAD A DREAM THAT CAME TRUE LATER?

56% Yeah, totally!
34% I think so, maybe
10% Not even

I have dreams about my crushes,

Yeah, yeah, yeah. Everyone's got a story about some kind of ESP in their dreams. Like people who dream about someone they've never met, then meet them a week later. Or whatever.

The thing is, dreams are almost impossible to verify. The problem? Dream content doesn't exist in the physical world, so it can't really be proved. So science has no way of matching up someone's dream with a real event. Plus, as soon as you wake up, your brain starts adding stuff into

but they never come true.—‹‹Kiwigirl››

your dream, editing other stuff out, coloring it, putting in logic where it didn't exist, and generally screwing with it.

So, could it happen? Sure, why not? There are many things in the world we don't understand. But if these dreams do happen, they're incredibly rare.

> I'VE HAD SOME VERY REALISTIC DREAMS COME TRUE MANY TIMES! SOME GOOD, SOME BAD. LIKE I DREAMED OF SOMEONE DYING ONCE, AND WHEN I WOKE UP THAT MORNING, WE RECEIVED A PHONE CALL SAYING THEY HAD! ALSO, I DREAMED ABOUT GOING OUT WITH THIS GUY I HAD A CRUSH ON AND THEN HE ASKED ME OUT, AND THE DATE WAS JUST LIKE IN THE DREAM!
>
> —JODIELYNN

RECURRING DREAMS

I have had the same dream almost every single night for as long as I can remember, even way back when I was a kid. It starts out with me floating around underwater, trying to figure out how to breathe. The water's really warm and gooey, almost like minty fresh tooth-whitening gel. When I can't think of a way to breathe, I stop trying and just suck in water. Whaddaya know, it works! I can breathe water!

I have it every night. Or practically every night. Okay, well, it feels like it happens every night.

What's it mean? I'm sure a strict Freudian would have something to say about warm, gooey places and maybe something about being in the womb. Jung might say something about preevolutionary primordial ooze and the emergence of life. Some might say I'm just holding my breath in my sleep and this is my little dream about it.

I, personally, have not figured it out to my satisfaction yet. All I know is that I have it all the time!

It's obviously trying to tell me something important. Maybe it's a message I just haven't clued into yet. (Something like, "You're doing everything wrong! Stop using logic, and start using your instinct!") Or maybe it's a message that I need to be reminded of every night. (Something like, "Don't hold your breath in your sleep, you moron!")

Recurring dreams happen to everyone. Pay attention to them. There's definitely something in them that your brain thinks is worth rewinding and playing back over and over. A confidence boost, or a piece of advice, or a warning. Listen up.

again.—Charlotte Barnard, "I Cannot Sing the Old Songs"

Lucid Dreams

You know how sometimes you'll be dreaming along, but it's like you know you're dreaming? You're all, "Hey! I'm dreaming! This rules!" It's like your conscious mind is checking it all out and saying, yeah, things are weird, but it's cool because we're dreaming here.

There's a name for it: lucid dreaming.

All together now: lucid dreaming.

What's it all about? Well, it's kind of like dragging your conscious mind along with you through a dream. Or maybe it's more like instant messages zipping between your conscious and unconscious mind while you're dreaming. It usually happens by accident, when something in your dream is just so out there and unbelievable that something clicks and your conscious mind starts paying attention. It might happen that you're dreaming along and you realize, "I know I am dreaming, and I like it."

It's a bizarre sensation, as anyone will tell you. If it happens in a happy dream, you get positively giddy. All, "Dang, being a super-model really is all that!" or, "Flying rules!" But if it happens in a nightmare, lucidity can be terrifying. Like, "I really, really wish I could run a little faster because that ax-murdering Carson Daly is closing in on me!" It's important to remind yourself during lucid dreams that it's your butt in the director's chair.

Lucid dreaming happens pretty randomly, from what we know, but some people say you can train yourself to have lucid dreams. Why would you want to? To experience things you can't do in real life, or to face fears you're too scared to deal with in real life, or whatever. But learning how, I mean really getting it down, means you'd probably have to do some major dream therapy. You know, since you have all those extra thousands of dollars lying around.

But until your first million comes in, try this: Every waking hour of the day, on the hour, ask yourself, "Am I dreaming?" Every hour. Set an alarm if you have to. Eventually, if you're lucky, it'll become a habit, one that your brain will still do when you're sleeping. And eventually, if you're really lucky, you'll ask yourself, "Am I dreaming?" when you're dreaming. And you'll answer, "Yes." Voilà! You're aware while you're in your dream.

Good luck.

> I HAD THIS DREAM THE OTHER DAY
> WHERE I ATE THIS PIECE OF CAKE, BUT AS SOON AS I
> FINISHED, IT REAPPEARED. I KEPT THINKING,
> "I HOPE THIS DOESN'T END. . . . THIS DREAM IS TOO
> MUCH FUN." IT WAS LIKE I KNEW I WAS DREAMING.
> —ZAZOU22

I knew that I dreamed.—Daphne du Maurier, Rebecca

How Come I Had the Exact Same Dream as My Friend Last Night?

You're freaking because you had a dream where your chem teacher went to your house and dropped a test on your class. You tell your lab partner about it, and she looks at you like you're Kathie Lee Gifford and screams, "Omigod, I had that same dream!"

The two of you stare at each other, hum the theme song to *The X-Files,* slap a high five, and go on with class.

But you think about it for the rest of the day.

Here's the deal: You didn't have the same dream. What you had are two incredibly similar dreams, but each was unique. You both had a lot of the same raw material to work with—you're in the same class, you both want to get good grades, you both know there's a test in your not-too-distant future. So it's not so strange to think that you both could have come up with eerily similar dreams.

I know how he dreams me. I know because I

Even if you had less in common with the person who shared your dream, if you look hard enough, chances are that you two share some circumstance or characteristic that would produce similar dreams.

Now, this isn't to say that it couldn't happen. We are talking about dreams here, and there's so much we don't understand that I guess anything is possible. But I feel confident in saying it straight up wasn't the exact same dream.

a different point of view

Some dream researchers say that people can and do have the same dreams all the time. They say that we exchange information back and forth between our unconscious minds without our conscious minds even knowing it. In other words, the dream you had that was the same as someone else's could have been "planted" in your unconscious mind without you or the "planter" even knowing it.

Lots of people say they had the same dream as a friend, especially when they've slept in the same room or bed together. Did they exchange information unconsciously the night before? Perhaps. Or did they just have the same stuff on their minds when they went to sleep since they hung out together before crashing? Who knows?

dream his dreams.—Rosellen Brown, "How to Win"

Dying in Your Dreams Means You'll Die in Real Life, and Other Total Lies

Here's the deal: Real-life rules do not apply to dreams. That's why you get to fly, win a Best New Artist Grammy, be really mean to people who would kick your ass in real life, morph into a wild animal, be naked all over town, stuff like that. It's this lack of rules that makes dreaming so cool and so scary.

So when you die in your dreams, it doesn't mean you're going to die. It doesn't mean you're in danger of dying. It doesn't mean you want to die. It doesn't even mean you're afraid of dying. Same goes when someone else dies in your dreams or even when you kill someone in your dreams. Death in dreams signifies change and transition.

(Oh, and don't be surprised if someone dies in your dreams and you don't get upset by it. Happens to me all the time. I asked a pro, and it's completely normal.)

Most of the time if you die in your dreams, it means that part of you is going through some major changes. Like if you're getting rid of that part of you that's scared of the dark or that part of you that gets pissed when your kid brother spills Coke on your sweater. In other words, you're changing or "killing off" parts of your personality.

A dreamer lives for eternity.

Finding other people dead in your dreams, or watching them die, or killing them means that the part of you they represent is going through some changes.

That's why teenagers have so many dreams about death. There's a lot of change going on, a lot of "killing off" of those childhood characteristics and fears. And let's face it, those are some of the scariest dreams going.

Don't bug. You're not about to die. Remember, dreams don't make sense.

Other Major Dream Misconceptions

If I have sex with someone in my dream, does it mean I want to do it with them in real life?
No.

If I hook up with someone of the same sex in my dream, does that mean I'm gay?
No.

If I cheat on my significant other in my dream, does that mean I want to cheat on 'em in real life?
No.

If I'm really harsh on someone in my dream, does it mean that deep down I hate them?
No.

If I commit a crime in my dream, does that mean I'm a bad person?
Nope.

If I do something weird in my dream, does it mean I'll do it in real life? Does it mean I want to do it in real life?
No. No.

—Anonymous

Seriously Insane Dreams. They're Seriously Normal.

So you wake up at around 5 A.M. in a minipanic, and you realize you just had a dream in which you totaled your dad's car, then jumped into someone's minivan, picked up a hitchhiker who turned out to be Drew Barrymore, cut off all her hair, then started making out with her till she turned into a gopher, at which point you put her on a stick and cooked her over a campfire. Oh, and you were wearing nothing but tie-dyed socks the whole time.

Bizarre? Yep. Disturbing? Maybe. Cause for concern? Not even.

Okay, what about dreams where you dismember your grandparents? Normal.

Dreams where you have sex with Pamela Anderson Lee? Normal.

Dreams where you win a gold medal, then give the finger to the camera during your interview? Normal.

Dreams where someone reads your tarot cards and predicts your death the next day? Totally normal.

Dreams where you show up butt naked to gym class and your gym teacher turns out to be T-Boz? Normal.

See, no matter how weird your dreams are, they're no weirder than anyone else's. Think of the sanest person you know. That person has seriously whacked-out dreams. Now, think of the craziest person you know. That person also has seriously whacked-out dreams. Seeing a pattern?

We all have messed-up situations happening in our heads all night long (and all day long, too, but that's another book). You can do things and experience things in your dreams that just don't happen, and shouldn't happen, in real life.

When you do need to get worried is when you start having extremely disturbing dreams so regularly that you can't sleep well. Or when your dreams are so intense every night that they're haunting you, keeping you from being happy during the day. In other words, when your dreams are so major that they really take a toll on the rest of your life, speak to someone about it. A parent, counselor, clergy person, coach, friend, whatever. There are ways to deal with it. You deserve (and need) a decent night's sleep.

> SOMETIMES, EVEN THOUGH I'M A GIRL . . .
> IN MY DREAM I'M A GUY. OR I SWITCH FROM
> CHARACTER TO CHARACTER IN MY DREAMS, AND
> FOR EACH CHARACTER I FEEL AS THEY WOULD
> FEEL AND SEE WHAT THEY WOULD SEE.
> —DAYNERS

Famous Dreamers

Okay, this whole dream thing is interesting and all, but dreams don't really seem all that useful, right? Well, you're right and you're wrong. For most people, even people who pay attention to their dreams, dreams kind of go along, often in the background of their lives. Analyzing dreams is fun and all, but so is watching TV or chatting on-line.

But most of us have had at least one or two dreams in our lives that we just can't shake, dreams that stuck with us because we sensed they had some message for us. And believe it or not, for many people dreams and the information culled from them have been downright helpful.

Check it out:

WILLIAM SHAKESPEARE (1564–1616) packed the house and made some cash at the end of the sixteenth century with his comedy *A Midsummer Night's Dream,* which is all about finding truth in dreams instead of in reality. Dreams also play big parts in many of his other plays, such as *Julius Caesar, Richard III,* and even *Romeo and Juliet.* His inspiration? His own dreams.

MARY SHELLEY (1797–1851) came up with the idea for her novel *Frankenstein* in her dreams. It was published in 1818 and remains one of the most popular novels of all time. Thanks to Mary's dreams, hundreds of moviemakers and actors have cashed in over the years.

Unlimited and absolute is the vision of him who sits at ease and

INVENTOR ELIAS HOWE (1819–1867) said one inspiration for his invention—the sewing machine—came from a nightmare he had about being attacked by cannibals bearing spears that looked exactly like the needle he then designed.

PAINTER SALVADOR DALÍ (1904–1989) used to wake himself up from dreams and immediately paint what he'd just been dreaming about. Ever seen his work? It's as surreal and dreamy as art can get.

watches, who walks in loneliness and dreams.—Oscar Wilde

CARLOS CASTANEDA (1931–1998) used dreams and what he learned about them from a Yaqui Indian wise man to write *The Teachings of Don Juan: A Yaqui Way of Knowledge,* an incredibly controversial book that earned Castaneda full-on cult hero status and plenty of cash. It's one of the trippiest books of all time.

According to rock legend, Keith Richards woke up one morning humming the riff to "Satisfaction." He wrote it down, Mick Jagger laid down a vocal, and one of the biggest hits in rock history was born.

Bottom line? You may not wake up and write the rock anthem of the century based on a dream, and you may not transform the textile industry after a great sleep; but if you look hard enough, there may be some answers in those dreams of yours. Info that could help you produce the greatest novel of all time—or at least understand yourself a little better.

If you think about something long enough before

dream incubation

In many cultures throughout history—from ancient Mesopotamia and India right up to present-day New York City—people have figured that if you ask the right questions and perform the right rituals before going to sleep, your dreams will hit you up with answers to problems that you're facing in real life. Does it work? Who knows? Try it yourself: Write down your problem just before going to sleep, then stick it under your pillow. If it's floating around your brain while you're crashing, your chances of having a revealing dream about your problem just might go up.

going to bed, you can dream about it.—‹‹mathwig››

The Science Part

Okay, concentrate! Here comes the science part!

WHEN DO DREAMS HAPPEN?

Believe it or not, you pretty much dream all night long. Some of your dreams are like channel surfing, though—you see an image or two, but they don't really make an impact and you don't remember them. But a few times a night, every night, you come across a really good show. And those dreams can last for quite a while.

Here's the deal: We don't understand sleep or dreaming all that well. But we have managed to break down a night's sleep into five different stages or categories. We call them stage 1, stage 2, stage 3, stage 4, and stage 5 (or REM). Took a genius to come up with those names!

HERE'S THE BREAKDOWN

Stage 1 sleep happens right after you nod off. It lasts for a few minutes. Not a lot happens. Your brain's just kind of winding down, zoning out, replaying the day in your head, stressing out about the midterm tomorrow, trying to figure out why your best friend is such a freak sometimes, and stuff like that. Any dreams you have during this stage are pretty much just like daydreams.

Stage 2 happens next. You know how all of a sudden your body jerks, you barely notice it, and you fall into a deeper sleep almost right away? That's when you're entering stage 2. Stage 2 sleep is slightly deeper than stage 1

Even sleepers are workers and collaborators in

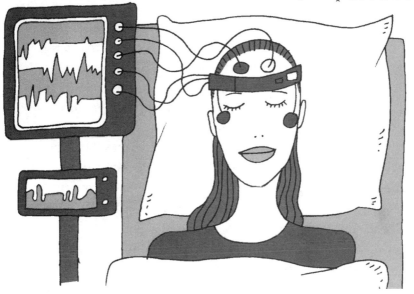

sleep—as your decreasing brain activity proves.

Stage 3 sleep is a lot like stage 2 sleep but deeper. Unless you're a psychophysioanalyst or something, there's not much to distinguish between the two.

Stage 4 sleep is the deepest. Brain activity, while it doesn't ever stop, really slows down. This is the sleeping-like a log phase. Not a lot of dreaming happens during this stage.

REM sleep (stage 5) is the final stage. No, not the band. This is the most active sleep stage, which is kind of an oxymoron since you're asleep and supposed to be resting, but hey.

REM stands for rapid eye movement. If you watch someone in the REM stage, you'll see their eyeballs darting back and forth really fast underneath their eyelids. But it's not

what goes on in the universe.—Heraclitus, Fragments

just the eyeballs that are going nuts. Your hormones start partying, your pulse rate goes up, and you start breathing more heavily, taking in more oxygen. Oh, and you start dreaming, hard.

REM sleep is when the most vivid dreams happen. The visuals are much more exciting, the emotions are more intense, and you're more likely to remember these dreams. Luckily your muscles are shut down during this period, so you can't react to your dreams physically—as in, running off a cliff or attacking your Chem teacher with a Bunsen burner. At least not usually.

On the downside, because REM sleep is so active, older people can suffer heart attacks, people at risk for seizures and asthma suffer more attacks, and we all produce a little

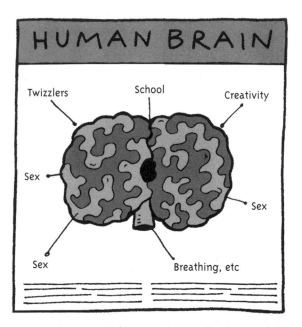

extra gas. Fun!

Your first REM session of the night lasts a few minutes. Then you're bumped back down to stage I and the whole cycle starts over again. The routine happens six or so times during the night (it's amazing you get any rest at all!), and each time you hit REM, it lasts for a bit longer. By the end of the night you can spend up to an hour straight in REM.

WHAT HAPPENS TO MY BRAIN WHEN I DREAM?

Okay, concentrate. First, know this: The brain is such a whacked-out place that no one really understands it at all, no matter what they tell you. All we can do is measure what's measurable—like brain activity, chemical reactions, and stuff like that—but that doesn't mean we really get it at

How Long Do Dreams Last?

You're sitting there telling a friend about a dream you had, but all you can come up with is one image. The next day you're talking about another dream, and you might as well be reciting War and Peace, the dream is so intricate and long. What's the deal?

Some dreams really are only a quick image or sensation. Those dreams might last a few seconds or even less. Some dreams, especially REM dreams, are way more detailed and longer. Like a half hour or more.

One thing's for sure—dream time has very little to do with real-life time. In a dream entire lives can be lived in just a few seconds, and washing your face can take what seems like forever.

comprehends more than it can coordinate.—Vauvenargues

all. It's a big ol' mystery, especially the sleeping brain.

But hey, that's not gonna stop me from oversimplifying everything. Here goes:

Brain Waves

If you wanted to hook yourself up to an electroencephalograph (EEG) while you were sleeping, just for laughs, say, you would see that your brain is incredibly active all night long. An EEG measures brain activity, called brain waves (which aren't really waves at all, but whatever). So your brain is busy thinking, controlling your organs and muscles, producing hormones, all that stuff.

While you're sleeping, your EEG readings will peak and

jerk your body

There you are, peacefully drifting off, all snuggled up, falling to sleep bit by bit, when bam! Your whole body jerks, practically lifting you off the bed. You hit full consciousness for about one second before falling immediately into a deeper sleep. Sound familiar?

Happens to me all the time. It's your nervous system sending one more shout out before chilling out for the night. Kind of like how when you unplug your stereo all of a sudden, there's a last burst of energy and some feedback from the speakers before it shuts down.

Lots of us create dreams to coincide with the jerk. Me, I often dream about slipping on a patch of ice. A friend of mine dreams about getting shot in the head. Okay, so he's kind of weird. Anyway, next time you're woken up by the jerk, force yourself to stay awake. Ask yourself: Were you dreaming when it happened?

The human mind is not meant to be governed, certainly

plummet all night long, depending on what stage of sleep you're in. In stage I sleep the readings would look a lot like they do when you're awake. During deeper stages EEG activity slows down. But during REM sleep it goes nuts.

Chemicals

When you hit REM sleep, your brain eases up on producing the chemicals (norepinephrine and serotonin) that help it deal with senses like taste, smell, and the ability to feel physical pain. (Hey, give it a break—it's sleeping.) Since these chemicals aren't buzzing around your head you can't taste, smell, or physically feel anything much at all.

To make things interesting while those chemicals are kicking back, a new, multitasking chemical called acetylcholine revs up. This is a chemical that (a) encourages your brain to order up physical motion, (b) basically paralyzes your muscles at the same time, and (c) boosts your emotions. Which would account for why you feel like so much is going on in your dream, but at the same time your body is lying there doing nothing. Oh, and that feeling you get when you're being chased in your dream and you really, really want to book but can't move your legs? Acetylcholine.

Feel like a science lab yet?

Anyway, that's what we know about what happens in the brain during dreams. Make sense? Cool. Still confused? You're in good company. Even the most advanced sleep researchers are confused, too. Science has really just scratched the surface of dreams, so while these are valuable pieces of the puzzle, it's far from complete.

not by any book of rules yet written.—Lewis Thomas

Sleepwalking

There's all kinds of stuff that people do in their sleep that makes no sense. Like getting up and walking around. Or taking a shower. Or eating. Or dealing out a deck of cards. And I gotta say, it's pretty hilarious when you see your eleven-year-old brother heading straight for the Nintendo 64 two hours after he's gone to bed. It's like, dude—you're asleep. Get in bed and snore or something!

But it's also pretty freaky. There's no sense to what he's doing. So what's to keep him from jumping out the window or attacking me with the game console?

Here's the deal: No one really knows exactly why sleepwalking (or as sleep researchers call it, somnambulism) happens. But we do know some facts. Like it's way more common in kids than grown-ups. (No one really knows why.) It's way more common in boys than girls. (Again, no one knows exactly why.) It usually happens during the first few hours of sleep. Sleepwalking parents often have sleepwalking kids. It doesn't always have to do with a dream. Sleepwalkers almost never remember doing it. And it doesn't usually happen every night.

★ Alloy User Poll ★

DO YOU WALK IN YOUR SLEEP?

6% All the time
72% Never
22% I have no idea—
I'm asleep

Sleepwalking is usually harmless, but not always. The person doing it isn't really all that clued into things like logic and right and wrong, which can be dangerous. There have even been some reported cases of sleepwalkers walking in front of cars or climbing into their cars and driving off cliffs. (This is very rare, so please don't spend time worrying about it.) There've been murder cases where defendants have claimed they were sleepwalking and couldn't control their actions. Many a family member has been slapped across the face by a sleepwalker who really, really didn't mean it. Not nice.

If you or someone you know has a problem with sleepwalking, contact a sleep disorder center in your area or hit the American Academy of Sleep Medicine at http://www.asda.org.

is it dangerous to wake a sleepwalker?

No. In fact, it's not a bad idea. But do it gently, quietly, cautiously, and slowly. Nudge them back to bed or to reality with a soft touch. And duh, if they have a knife or are acting scary, get outta the way. Oh, and be nice and don't make fun of them in the morning. Even if they were sleepwalking in the nude.

dream.—Ralph Waldo Emerson, The Conduct of Life

OTHER RANDOM SLEEP DISORDERS

Sleep bruxism—when people grind or clench their teeth. Lots of people do this.

Sleep paralysis—when people can't move their bodies even after their brains have woken up. Sometimes this lasts only a few seconds, but sometimes it can last for several terrifying minutes.

Rhythmic movement disorder—when people rock back and forth all night long.

Periodic limb movement disorder (PLMD)—when people's arms and legs jerk around all night, sometimes clocking whomever they're sleepin' with.

Restless legs syndrome (RLS)—when people kick their legs back and forth . . . kinda like a sleeping dog. This can

★ Alloy User Poll ★

DO YOU TALK IN YOUR SLEEP?

26% All the time
17% Never
57% I have no idea
—I'm asleep

talking in your sleep

Everybody does it. No one ever remembers it. Some people do it all the time. Some people do it almost never. Some people laugh, cry, shout, sing, carry on major conversations. Others just sorta grunt and moan. I've been known to cuss in my sleep. And here's the strangest thing of all: It's not always associated with a specific dream. Sometimes sleep talkers are just, well, saying stuff. Like, "Didn't you finish making that Oreo pie yet?" and, "Hillary Clinton should definitely go on tour with TLC."

Let not our babbling dreams affright

last for several freaky minutes.

Narcolepsy—when people fall asleep uncontrollably, often at random times, like over lunch. Sounds funny, but what if you're driving your car?

Sleep hyperhydrosis—when people sweat hard, all night. Nice.

Check this: Sometimes these sleep disorders can trigger dream images. Like sleep bruxism can get you dreaming about your teeth. Sleep hyperhydrosis can get you dreaming about the sauna.

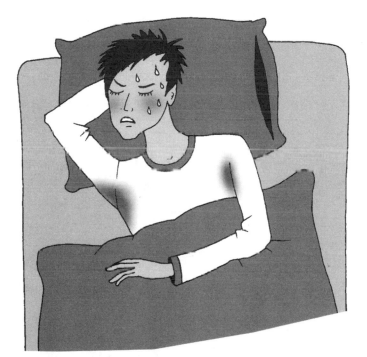

Babies Dream, Too!

Babies dream a lot. In fact, they probably dream a whole lot more than you and me put together. For one thing, babies up until a few months old sleep like fifteen or sixteen hours a day, right? That's twice as much as us. For another thing, because they're growing so fast, they need to sleep more deeply than we do, so they spend more than half their time in super dream-producing REM sleep. We're lucky if all our time in and out of REM sleep adds up to a couple of hours a night.

In other words, babies dream three or four more times more than we do.

So what exactly do they dream about? Well, they probably have a lot of dreams that are about feelings, about their senses. (They can't talk, after all.) Like a dream about being warm and cozy. Or a dream about hearing Mom's or Dad's voice.

Until they're a few months old, babies don't really have a firm grasp on what's a dream and what's not. So their dreams probably seem a whole lot more "real" to them than ours do.

In fact, even older kids—up to first or second grade even—have a hard time figuring it out when they're dreaming. That's why many kids wet the bed so much. You know, that whole I-was-in-the-bathroom-and-I-had-to-pee-really-bad-so-I-just-went-for-it dream, which we'd all like to forget.

We are such stuff as dreams are made on, and our little

Anyway, as babies get older, they probably start dream-ing about specific things they've encountered in the world, like that annoying multicolored mobile swinging over the crib, or graham crackers, or Grandma's superblond hairdo. What's more, their dreams even start to have stories. Not like *The Hobbit* or anything; more like, "I rolled over and it was fun," but hey, it's something.

life is rounded with a sleep.—Shakespeare, <u>The Tempest</u>

And they have nightmares—also called sleep terrors. Like about the way Mom yells when she gets mad at someone. Or being hungry. Remember—it's a scary world for an infant, no matter how well they're taken care of. Everything they see is new, unfamiliar, and way bigger than they are. Plus they can't do a whole lot but sit there or maybe scream in an emergency. So they've got a lot of material for nightmares.

But since babies can't talk, they can't really tell us about 'em, can they?

Do Blind People Dream?

*L*ike I said before, everyone dreams. People who've been blind from birth dream about feelings, sensations, sounds, ideas, stuff like that. You know, instead of visual stuff.

One must remember that both wild things and men

Do Pets Dream?

I f you have to ask, you probably don't own a pet. Otherwise you'd have seen that back leg kicking wildly or felt that extra-happy purr in the middle of the night and known exactly what was going on. Most mammals experience REM sleep, and many animals exhibit physical signs of dreaming, so it's a safe bet they dream. But since we can't really ask, we don't know for sure.

If they do dream, chances are they dream about something that recently happened to them—like chewing up that Frisbee or having to howl for dinner. They probably dream about really basic concepts, like running. Or breathing. Or Puppy Chow.

are animals . . .—Helen Hoover, "The Resident Birds"

every week at Alloy.com,

I read hundreds of e-mails about people's weird dreams, and every week I pick one to analyze on the site. It's a great job—dreaming is my favorite thing to do in the world, and this way I get to share other people's dreams, too.

And lemme just say that y'all have some really, really weird dreams. I mean, really weird.

But it's all good, and I've picked out a few of the weirdest to share with you.

So read on for a glimpse into the illness that is dreaming.

"I HAVE SOME REALLY GREAT SPACESHIP
DREAMS. BEING SHOT UP IN A CAPSULE
AND ENDING UP FLYING, OUT IN THE UNIVERSE,
OVER THE MOST BEAUTIFUL LANDSCAPES.
IT'S SO INTENSE. I HAVE CRAZY DREAMS ALL THE TIME."
—MILLA JOVOVICH, TO *NYLON* MAGAZINE

The One Where I Kiss My BF, Then I Get Hit by a Truck

Okay, I dreamed I was in my boyfriend's car, and we were driving on one of our local streets (I dreamed this the day after we first made out). I turned to him and said, "Do you like the way I kiss?" (I've only kissed one person before him), and he said, "No, maybe you need some practice!" and started frenching me right while we were in the middle of an intersection. Then while we were doing this (I wasn't viewing this all in first person—it was like my view was from the backseat), I see this huge truck about to hit us. I try to scream, and he gets upset that I'm trying to pull away from his kiss, like I don't like him or something. So he gets out just in time, and I'm still in the car, and then everything turns white. Then I woke up.   —Frenchkiss

★   ★   ★

Hmmm. Worried about your kissing abilities, are you? Here's what's what. That car you were in represents your experience with your boyfriend. It represents your relationship. The fact that he was driving means you feel like he's mostly in control of the relationship, that he's calling most of the shots.

Remember that everything in your dreams is created by your mind. So your boyfriend in your dream isn't actually your

I dreamed I was in a department store and I

boyfriend but a reflection of you and your feelings about him. If it seems like you felt a little insecure with him in the dream, you probably feel a little insecure around him in real life. Especially when it comes to kissing. Do you feel like he's more experienced than you are?

Your car, symbolizing your relationship, got slammed by a truck just after you started kissing. He got out all right, but for you, everything went to white. White in dreams symbolizes purity and peace but also emptiness. So after pressuring you to make out, he disappeared, and you were surrounded by emptiness.

I don't know, buttercup, it sounds to me like you're worried that this guy wants more from you physically than you're ready to give. Plus you feel like if you give it to him, your relationship will, well, get run over by a truck. Sounds like you don't feel so comfortable with this guy. Give some thought to where you want to go with your relationship.

kept yelling out really loud, "I am a 34B!"—‹‹zonda››

The One Where Mushrooms Grow Out of My Face

Here's the weirdest dream I've had in a while. I dreamed I was getting out of the shower and when I wiped the steam off the mirror I saw something way gross growing on my face! I looked closer and it was a patch of tiny mushrooms growing on my cheek. I started picking and scrubbing them off, but that only made more, bigger ones pop up. I was starting to panic, and I dunked my head into a sink full of water and used soap and everything I could find. I yelled for someone to help me, but I was home alone. When I tried to get out of the bathroom, the door had disappeared and I was trapped. I kept picking them off and pus would ooze out of them—it was too gross to describe. But then I woke up and my face was as clear as ever.   —FungiGirl

★   ★   ★

How totally disgusting. Anyway, let's take a look at what it means. When you're looking at yourself in the mirror in a dream, you're really looking at how you present yourself to the world. You know, your looks, your personality, your social behavior, your sense of humor, stuff like that. You're looking at what you think the rest of the world sees when they look at you and how confident you are.

I was wearing a long white dress and talking to a crocodile.

Okay, so, you see mushrooms all over your face. It seems pretty clear that on some level, you're afraid that the image you project to the world—be it your looks or your social behavior—is not all you want it to be. You don't feel bad about all of it; maybe only a little teeny part.

What's more scary is the fact that the more you get rid of the mushrooms, the more they grow. They keep sprouting up, getting bigger and more grotesque. That means there's yet another insecurity going on—deep down, you may be afraid that anything you do to try to improve your image (looks, behavior, etc.) will actually make it worse.

Have you gotten a new haircut lately that you hate? Or maybe bought some new clothes that just don't work? Or maybe you've started hanging with some new and different people. Perhaps there's someone you're crushing on, and you're not confident about their feelings.

This dream doesn't mean you're a freak. At all. Everyone in the whole, entire universe is self-conscious about the way they look—even supermodels and Olympic athletes and movie stars and all those peeps. It's part of being human. But this dream does mean you should take a minute to celebrate the stuff about you that does rock. You know, the nonmushroom parts.

In fact, I was queen of the crocodiles.—‹‹LauraVe››

The One Where I Wear an Outfit Made of Glitter

Okay, I was walking through this hall in my school. It's one of those outside halls that has a roof, and in real life the hall isn't that long, but in my dream it seemed to go on forever. Anyway, I was walking down the hall, asking everyone if they had any glitter they could spare. And I was collecting it in this jar. I got glitter from all kinds of people, like my mom, and people I haven't seen or talked to in years. Then I noticed I was wearing a utility suit made of glitter. What's the deal?

—GlamRock

★　　★　　★

Let me guess. You want to be a dancer in Vegas or a figure skater, what with all the glitter.

Just kidding.

So you were walking

I dreamed I was running laps around my school

down a long hallway . . . In fact, "it seemed to go on forever." Long hallways in dreams usually mean that in your real life you're anxious about something coming up, like a big date, or a test, or a competition, or something like that. An event where you'll have to perform, or be really cool, or look great, or whatever. The hallway represents your anxiety about what's coming up.

As you were walking down the hallway, you were collecting glitter, and lots of it. Collecting things in your dreams also usually means that you're getting ready for something big in your real life, that you're getting together everything you'll need to deal.

Hmmm. You were collecting glitter. What's that about? Glitter makes people stand out, makes them look special, different, even a little kooky. You gotta be pretty confident to wear a whole lot of glitter. The glitter in your dream represents confidence, which you were collecting from all kinds of different people, including your mother and people you haven't seen in years. In other words, you were leaning on others for support as you anticipate this upcoming event (whatever it is).

Congratulations. This dream means that you've figured out, subconsciously, how to be successful—it's by looking to those who love you and those who have loved you in the past (those people you haven't seen in years) for help and support. Deep down, no matter how stressed you might feel, you truly believe you'll be all right. And totally glittered out.

but then it turned into a Coke machine.—‹‹Alvin››

The One Where I Get Chased by Coyotes!

My dream starts out in the field behind my house. It's midnight, and my friend and I are waiting for her boyfriend and his friend. We're getting scared because we've been out there awhile. I turn around to look for them, and I see coyote eyes staring back at me. I yell to my friend to run. We start to run, but there's a barbed wire fence in my way. I jump it, but my friend isn't so lucky.

I turn around because I realize she's not behind me. The coyotes have eaten her alive! I get scared and I know I can't do anything for her, so I run to my house. I look out the window and see the coyotes circling my house. I've heard that if a person has had a dream three times in a row, it will more than likely come true. I've had my dream three times. Please tell me what this means!   —Howler

★   ★   ★

If you dream something three times, it will not come true. That is a myth. But it does mean you need to pay attention.

You're out in a field. That's important. Wide-open spaces in your dreams represent your whole world, your whole life.

It's night, making your dream scary; ominous. You're waiting for people who aren't showing up, which probably means you're waiting for part of yourself to make things okay. Which part? Maybe it's your sense of morality, maybe your logical

I had this dream that I was at my

mind, maybe your brilliant creativity—whatever will save you.

But instead wild animals show up and start chasing you! They represent your own scariest emotions . . . the ones that creep up behind you and bite you. They get your friend, which means they've already got the part of you that you most closely associate with her.

You make it to your house before the coyotes do. This means that in real life when those wild-animal emotions creep up, you can find a place in your brain that's safe—like home. But just because you're out of immediate danger doesn't mean those emotions disappear.

Okay, put it all together. You're out there in your life, try-ing to get part of your brain to kick in, when all these emo-tions get in the way and you run and hide.

The good news is, since you're still aware of the emotions while you're in your house, it means you can put your brain to work making them less scary, making them work for you.

Great dream. It seems scary, but it's actually pretty hopeful.

The One Where My Parents Throw Me Off a Cliff

I have this dream whenever I'm sick and whenever I've had a bad day. It begins with me on top of a cliff. I'm looking down the cliff, and there's a waterfall beside me. I turn around, and my mom and dad are right behind me, but they look like giants, like they're ten feet tall. Then they pick me up and drop me over the cliff. Somehow I live, and I go over to the waterfall and my sister is there. She hands me a key and tells me to go away. Can you please help me with this odd dream? I've been having this dream since I was a little girl.

—BadDayGirl

★   ★   ★

Recurring dreams like that are such a trip. Every time you have it, part of your brain is all, "Oh, this again," and part of your brain is like, "Omigod! This again!" and still another part of your brain could be seeing it for the first time. But since it happens all the time, it's really important to pay attention to it.

Being on top of a big cliff like that usually means you're frightened of something in real life. But instead of making a dream about what you're really anxious or fearful about, that wacky thing you call a brain makes up a dream about something completely different but just as scary and dangerous.

Your parents toss you over the cliff. This doesn't mean they're out to get you in real life. But whatever your parents

I had a dream that I was at school,

represent (probably authority or something) is what's going to make you face the fear that the cliff represents. They just won't let you turn around and walk away from the cliff.

You go over the waterfall, you survive (very important!), and there's your sister, holding a key. Keys almost always symbolize a solution or an answer. So you see your sister (or what she represents, and only you know what that is) holding the answer to the dilemma represented by the cliff.

I'd say that since you were a little girl, you've been afraid of something very basic and inevitable—something as basic as growing up. Your parents, or what they represent, are responsible for making you face whatever it is that's scaring you. You face it, and you survive. And after your safe landing, you notice that your sister, who's facing the same dilemma, seems to have a better clue of how to deal with it.

The One Where All My Teeth Fall Out

I keep having these really vivid nightmares that my teeth fall out! To make a lot of long stories short . . . it's usually all of them, but if all of them don't come out, the rest of them are all broken and rotten with exposed nerve endings and intense pain.

I used to think I had these dreams because my wisdom teeth were bothering me and were hurting in my sleep, but they haven't hurt for months, and I still have these dreams. Sometimes they fall out and bleed, and I try to keep them so I can try to get them to a dentist and put back into my head, and sometimes they're really loose, so I just pull them out with no difficulty.

In nightmares when I pull them out, I'll look in the

mirror and still see my teeth, but then they turn sideways or start to rot! These dreams really freak me out!!! Why do you think I keep having nightmares about my teeth?

—Toothless

I dreamed my mother was being stalked by

★   ★
★

Okay, first of all: Yuck. There. Now. Did you know that dreams about your teeth falling out are some of the most common dreams going? Yep, people dream about losing their teeth or about having really gross teeth situations all the time.

Here's what it's about: control. See, teeth represent power and control. Ever since the days of the caveman, they've been really important to us: We eat with them, we talk with them, we use them to scare off people or animals that are attacking us, we bite off store tags with them, stuff like that. And we take really good care of them, or at least we try to. (Right?)

In other words, we all have a very close relationship to our teeth. They help us control our lives, and in turn we control them very closely. So it's all about control.

Now, when they start to fall apart in your dream, it means you're feeling like you're losing control over some important aspect in your life, an aspect that you should be in charge of. Maybe you're letting grades slip somewhere. Maybe you've told a lie, and now it's coming back to haunt you. Maybe you accepted responsibility for something you really don't want to deal with.

Take a look at what's up in your life. Smart money says there's something you've lost control of.

Now, go floss.

The One Where I Hated My Party Outfit

I had this really weird dream, about a dance that I was going to. I got there, it was at my friend's house, and it ended up that I had on only my bathing suit and a really short T-shirt. Well, this was mortifying because I hate the way my legs look in a swimsuit!

Anyway, I only noticed it when I was dancing with the guy I was in love with at the time, and he said I shouldn't worry, that it was okay. I didn't agree, so I called my mom, but she wasn't there, and it ended up that she had forgotten to give me my shorts to put on over my suit, and she was on her way. She showed up, but I said that I wouldn't wear those shorts; I wanted a dress.

So we went home (not my house) and I got ready, which took forever. And then when we were going back, my mom wasn't in her car anymore; she was driving a station wagon now, and I had to ride on the tailgate to get back to the dance. Well, I couldn't convince her to go any faster, and when I got back to the

I dreamed my social studies teacher turned into

dance, almost everyone was gone and my friend's mom was handing out party favors! I can't figure out what this means! Help!   —Shopomatic

⋆ ⋆ ⋆

Two, two, two classic dream themes in one! Classic dream theme #1: Being underdressed.

Consider yourself lucky. Most people who have this kind of dream aren't just showing their legs; they're showing all the goods. If you know what I mean.

This reveals a fear of being exposed or of someone finding out something about you that you don't want them to know. In the dream you don't want your crush all scrutinizing your legs. While that may be true in real life as well, the dream probably means a little bit more: You don't want guys (symbolized by your crush) to know too much about your deeper, darker self (symbolized by your nudie-pudie legs). Why? Because you don't feel comfortable revealing it.

Which isn't the worst thing in the world.

Classic dream theme #2: Being driven around by someone going too slow.

Most times cruising around in a car in your dream represents cruising through life. The only problem is, in your dream it's being driven by your mother, not you, and she's not going nearly fast enough for you to reach your goal—the party. So probably in your real life you feel (way down deep) that the stuff your mother represents (most likely authority, but also possibly morality) is keeping you from blazing through life the way you want to.

Think it over. And be glad you at least had on a bathing suit!

The One Where Me and My Family Almost Drown

I've been having dreams every so often about huge waves from the sea. They're normally nightmares. Last night I had a dream that my sister had gone to this place on the beach with my cute little dog and that she couldn't get back 'cause the tide was in and there were giant waves. I was standing on this rock, screaming and crying for her, shouting her name out loud, but she was nowhere to be seen. A while ago I had a dream that I was walking along the beach and it got very late and it was time to get back home, and as I was walking, the waves got extremely big and I had to get very close to the cliffs and the waves got bigger and stronger each time I kept trying to go, and sometimes they would grab me but I would be just able to get out of them. Could you please explain to me why it is that I keep having dreams about huge waves and the sea?

—Surfergirl

★ ★ ★

This is the kind of dream that surfers, well, dream about. But for you, it's not cool. It's scary.

What's it mean? Quite simply, it's about emotional upheaval.

See, in dreams the ocean usually represents the vast unconscious mind that you have up there in your head. It seems so big because your mind is so big—it can think and do and imagine anything. Huge.

I had a dream that I was No Doubt's new

If the ocean in your dream were calm, that would mean your unconscious brain is calm. But dangerous, threatening waves mean that there's trouble a-brewin' up there. Both of the dreams you mentioned have to do with feeling trapped by the waves—in one case, it's people you love being threatened and you being unable to do anything about it, and in the other case, it's you being directly threatened. Either way, the rough seas of your unconsciousness, the emotional storm that's going on, is getting in the way of you being able to deal.

What's it all mean? Well, duh. You've got a lot on your mind—not just in your conscious mind, but in your unconscious mind, also, that's troubling and traumatic and even scary. The good news: Having dreams like this, even nightmares, helps you process and deal with all the chaos. It helps release some of the anxiety and negative energy.

In the meantime check your head and start to identify what things are churning up these big waves. Eventually they'll start to settle down.

drummer but I couldn't find the band anywhere.—‹‹devon››

The One Where My Girlfriend Died

I don't think that this dream is funny at all, but I really want to know what it's supposed to mean. Well, I dreamed that my girlfriend died in a car accident, and I felt awful. Then out of nowhere all of these girls were trying to act and dress just like my girlfriend (these girls were like model types) and asking me on dates. I was like, "Heck, no!" And I pushed them away. Then I woke up. What does this mean? —Dan-o

I dreamed this big dog got all in

So, here's the deal: Dreaming that someone you care about dies doesn't mean they're going to die or that you kind of want them to die.

It could mean that there are some changes going on in your relationship with her. Death in dreams signifies change.

The good part comes when you see all the other chicas start trying to get with you. That says you're confident that you'd be able to have other girlfriends if you needed to. But the really good part is when you turn 'em all down, even though they're model types and are going all out trying to be like her. What that says is that you know your girlfriend is way special and way unique and that even if all the other girls in town tried to be exactly like her, you'd know perfectly well that the real thing is all that counts.

To me that says the change you're going through is that you two are getting closer. Your casual relationship is "dying" to make room for a more intense one. Somewhere way down deep, you might be feeling that you're ready to go to another level with her.

It might also mean that somewhere you're worried she's going to make an exit outta your life. Which isn't such an unusual thing to feel, especially with a girlfriend or boyfriend, no matter how secure the relationship. It means you really care about her.

Sounds like your relationship is pretty tight, man. Go give your GF a big, fat kiss.

The One Where David Boreanaz Made Out with Me

It started when I was in the jungle with the old *Saved by the Bell* cast, and we were swinging on trapezelike swings. Until there was a storm and it sucked us down. I landed on a tree house in the middle of a lake. It was a big barbecue, but all of a sudden there was a huge rainstorm and everyone jumped in a boat and rode to safety—but I was stuck on the house. So all the boats were gone and I was left by myself, surrounded by water. The choices I had were to jump in the water and drown or stay on the house while it sank, like *Titanic*, and drown. So I slid down a wall and had started crying when I heard a boat. I wiped the tears away and looked around. And there I saw David Boreanaz in his little undershirt driving a boat toward the house. He stopped right in front of an exit and held out his hand for me to get in. So I hopped in and held on tight to his waist. Then when we got to safety, he grabbed me and kissed me like in a great fantasy. Then I woke up.   —Angelzgrl

★   ★
★

This dream is a clear indication that you watch waaaay too much TV.
Just kidding.

Once I dreamt that half of me turned into a witch

Let's see. You're hanging with some people, partying in the jungle, when all of a sudden this big storm comes along and leaves you alone. Frightened, you bug out. Until a romantic dude comes along and saves ya.

Hmmm. A jungle? That usually represents the most confusing, scariest part of your brain. And you're hanging out in there, swinging from the trees.

A major storm? That usually means there's some major chaos going down in your life. Since this storm happens in the jungle, your chaos is probably happening way down deep—maybe so deep that you're not even really conscious of it. Somewhere down there, you're really going through it.

A sinking ship? That usually means you're feeling some kind of personal failure.

Being cut off, alone? That usually means you feel like you have to deal with the situation all by your lonesome, that you feel you need to find the answers all by yourself.

David Boreanaz to the rescue? Romance fools like the answer to all your drama.

Throw it all together: You're struggling with some insecurity way down deep, and you're feeling isolated because of it. Your rescue? Tall, dark, and handsome—in an undershirt.

Think it over. But keep this in mind: David Boreanaz ain't no ticket to happiness. You gotta write your own.

The Ones Where All These Fires Keep Sprouting Up

When I was little, I had recurring dreams about fires—not raging fires, but small fires around the house. They were always in my grandpa's old house, and I would run around screaming for help and no one would listen to me. One time I lit the tips of my fingers on fire and was calling to a neighbor to help me, but she never turned around. Other times it would just be bundles of little fires all over the place and everyone just walking around not paying attention.

Only once the dream was at my house. It was during a party, and there was a fire, or rather a flame in a tree. It wasn't growing; it was just small. But I panicked and tried to tell my mom, but she wouldn't listen, she just kept saying, "That's nice," so I ran upstairs and called 911, but they wouldn't listen to me, either. This was the last dream I ever had like that. I know it isn't that weird, but I'd really like to know what the dreams meant.   —GiGgLeS

★   ★   ★

I don't know, GiGgLeS. I think you're selling yourself a little bit short—that sounds like a pretty weird dream to me.

I dreamed I had this branch, with leaves and

Anyway, here's the deal.

Your mom in your dream is most likely a part of yourself that your brain has decided to represent by using your mother. And your grandpa's old house is a feeling you have that your brain has decided to represent by using your grandpa's old house. Or whatever—you get the point.

Buildings, especially your own home and the homes of people you know and love, represent you. Walking through a house like this is like walking through your brain.

Fires usually represent some sort of chaos or destruction. Dreaming about fires (even "small ones") in your home means you're feeling chaos (even if it's small chaos) in your life.

What's interesting is that other people don't seem to notice or care. You are the only one alarmed.

If you ask me, and you did, I'd say you had these dreams at a time when you were feeling all kinds of chaos going on in your life but that no one was paying attention. Like, you were having problems and stuff, and no one was really helping you out.

The fact that you've stopped having these dreams could mean many things. Maybe you feel less chaos in your life. Or maybe you feel like people are supporting you more. Or maybe you've started having different dreams that express the same thoughts and feelings. Think about it.

stuff, growing out of my leg.—‹‹gazeboguy››

The One Where I Almost Get Squashed by a Lawn Chair

I have a recurring dream that I always get when I go to sleep really upset or something. In my dream I'm really little (like three inches tall), and I'm standing underneath a long line of lawn chairs that are folded up and are leaning against each other. All of a sudden one starts to fall and there's a domino effect and all the chairs are falling toward me. I just run as fast as I can, but I can't escape. What really scares me in the dream is the noise the chairs are making. When the first one falls, it's not too loud, but it quickly gets louder and louder. At the end of my dream the chairs are falling, but it always ends right before I get squashed.　　　　　—Tanya

★　　★　　★

Hmmm. Let's take a closer look here. Those chairs are big and scary, and they're towering over you all big and menacing. What's that about? Well, there's probably some obstacle in your life. A big one. (You said you have this dream whenever you go to bed upset, which is interesting—it's like even if the real-life obstacle changes, in your dream it's always represented by the chairs.) And compared to the obstacle, you see yourself as really small and helpless.

Anyway, they're big and scary. But when they start falling is when you really have to start dealing with them. As in, time's

I dreamed there was supposed to be a Korn

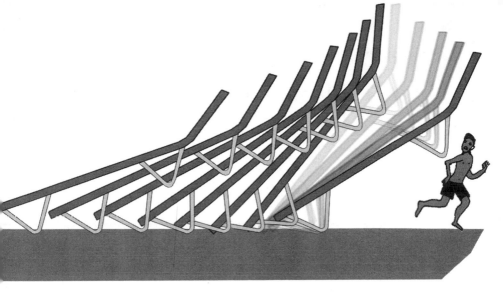

up. That means you're feeling helpless against your real-life obstacle—like it's going to get you no matter what you do. And soon.

The loud noise that's so scary is another indication that you feel like your obstacle is impossible to escape, just like a superloud noise is.

Luckily you wake up before getting squashed. Whew!

Although this sounds like a horrible dream, it isn't. It means that while you're sleeping, you're actually taking stock of the situation, figuring out how big and scary the obstacle really is. And allowing yourself to be helpless in your dream means that you won't have to be helpless in real life. It's like you deal with that part in dreamland, so you can meet your hurdles head-on in real life. See what I mean?

And the best news of all? You made yourself three inches tall, which means you can also make yourself ten feet tall.

The Ones Where I Leave Mom Behind

I've been having this dream where my mom and I are at a store. It's always dark outside. We're leaving, and my mom realizes that she left something in the store. So I go to the car without her.

I decide to start the car for my mom, and then I decide to start driving it. Well, I can't stop the car once it gets going. Then I see my mom coming out of the store, and I can't stop the car to pick her up. Sometimes I can't reach the brakes, or I don't know which pedal it is, or sometimes the brakes don't even work. I always start crying, and then the car will stop. But when she gets close to the car, it starts going again.

In all the years I've had this dream (since I was about five or six years old, and I'm fourteen now), I've never been able to pick her up. Sometimes the dream scares me a little. What does it mean?   —Momless

First of all, you gotta figure out what your mother was doing there in your dream. What does she represent in this dream? Safety? Comfort? Authority? Love?

Second, traveling in a car in your dream represents your journey through life. The fact that you decide to start driving the car is a good sign—it means you've decided to take control of your own life.

Your dream gets scary when you feel like you can't stop

In my dream these little people were sitting on potatoes while

the car (your life) to pick up your mother. You feel helpless because you can't figure out how to get her back in. You see her coming, but you just can't connect.

Looks like this dream is all about feeling a little bit afraid to move on with your life without the kind of love and safety that your mother could provide. It's waaaaaay normal. Everyone in the universe feels insecure about being able to stay in control without the help of parents.

But even if it's scary, the dream is a good one. It shows you've made the choice to call your own shots, and that you value and admire the good things your mother provides. The fact that somewhere deep down you're worried about not having her to help you every step of the way shows that you've already started figuring out how to deal alone

the microwave tray rotated around and around.—‹‹candyd››

.The One Where I'm Wearing Nothing but Price Tags

I had this dream that my best friend and I were trying on clothes at some store in the mall. I found this tight outfit that I wanted and went to ask for my friend's opinion. Anyway, I walked out of my dressing-room stall right into my school hall. I looked around trying to figure it out because it was summer vacation. Then all at once everyone there (the whole school) turned and looked at me. Everybody burst out laughing, so I looked down and noticed I was completely naked. The most odd thing was that I had price tags attached to my skin. I ran out of the school and ended up in my bed.   —Trine

★ ★ ★

Hey, Trine, right on. A classic hey-I'm-naked-here! dream. Trine style.

So you're in a mall, trying on a bunch of different clothes. In other words, you're looking at different ways to present your-self to the world. Experimenting with new options for expressing yourself.

I always have this dream where an ice cream truck crashes

So you find something, something tight fitting, that you want your friend to check out. It's a different look for you, and you'd like some feedback before rocking it in front of the whole world. (Remember, though, that it's not really your friend's approval you're looking for—it's part of you that you need an okay from.)

But argh! Before you can get some "safe" feedback from a bud, all of a sudden you're out there in front of the whole school. And all these people, who represent what-you-think-the-world-thinks-about-you, start cracking up. Why? Well, uh, because you're naked. Talk about the ultimate self-esteem buzz kill.

You'd think this would be a really easy I'm-self-conscious-about-my-body kind of dream, right? Wrong. See, even though you're bugging about the way you look in the dream, the self-consciousness in question could actually be about anything—from an upcoming date to how you'll get to that Warped concert next week to whether you're happy with your tan. Any kind of unsureness in your real life can turn into a naked dream.

Your solution in your dream was to climb back in bed. Will that be how you face your insecurities as they come up in real life?

Hope not.

P.S.—Price tags on your body? Now, there's an interesting twist. Sounds like on some level you consider your body to be another outfit to be "tried on" instead of the fantastic two-legged pod you're traveling through life in. Think about this, and work on treating your body with the respect, love, and care that it needs (and deserves).

into my yard . . . and the ice cream man is really hot.—‹‹jc››

The Ones Where My Crush Needs Wite-Out

Okay, here's how it goes. I keep having this dream almost every night. I'm at school and we're changing periods—and my crush comes up to me at my locker and asks me if I have any Wite-Out. I say, yeah, let me get it. So I go into my backpack and get my Wite-Out and go to give it to him, but he runs away! I really wouldn't think much of it, but I'm writing this 'cause it keeps getting freakier and freakier the more times I have it or even think about it. Can you help me and tell me what it means?

—Staples

Having the same dream over and over means there is something very important that your brain is trying to tell you. It's like seeing the same commercial over and over—they really want you to get the message.

So, the question is, what's the message?

You're at school. So this dream has to do with learning something. Some kind of lesson.

Your crush is there, so this dream has to do with a part of yourself that you like, a part that you want to get closer to.

So that part that you want to get closer to is asking you for Wite-Out. Like it wants to erase something or change something.

So you're in school (yes, back to learning), and part of you asks another part of you for some assistance in covering

I dreamed my boyfriend walked into the girls bathroom, dumped

something up. But before you can help, that part of you disappears, leaving you confused and useless.

Is there something about yourself (especially the part you project to other people) that you want to change or keep from other people but you can't? Think about it. You may be trying to force a change in yourself that goes against who you are as a person. Your dream is telling you not to bother—it won't work.

In other words, don't try to be something you're not.

The Ones Where I'm in a Video Game

My dream was that I was in a video game, and my family was there, too. There were lakes and rivers around, and I had to swing on vines to get across them. My family were back on land talking, and I was swinging over water to get to the land on the other side.

When I got over there, I went back over the water to talk to my family, and I couldn't cross over to the other side. I kept falling off the vine into the water. I didn't drown, but I couldn't cross over. I tried so many times, but I couldn't.

My dad was trying to help me but everyone else in my family was laughing. The really weird thing was that we were in a video game, so we were like animated. What does this mean?   —Donkey Kong

★   ★   ★

Here's the deal. You need to lay off the Nintendo. Just kidding. Or not. Whatever, that's none of my beeswax. Your dream, however, is. So let's get to it.

No doubt about it, this is about your relationship with your family. They're the only characters (besides you) in the dream.

But wait! You're all in the middle of a video game! Could this mean, somewhere deep down, that you feel your relationship with them is a kind of game? Something that requires strategy, dexterity, spontaneity, quick thinking. And oh yeah, a sense of humor? Hmmm.

I was going out with one of the 'N Sync guys. But then I cheated

There's more. You see them all hanging out together, chatting, laughing, staying in the same familiar place—while you're out there swinging around looking for new places to explore. But staying within their sight. Maybe like in real life, you're out there growing up, experiencing new things, having adventures, swinging around, but not getting so far away from your roots that you get totally lost.

Except in your dream you can't . . . quite . . . get . . . back . . . to . . . them. Your swinging around has isolated you. You've crossed water, for Pete's sake, which represents major milestones. Or barriers, depending on how you look at them.

(Think about making out for the first time. Your mother might think it's cute. Your dad might think it's dangerous. Or vice versa.)

So you're over there, isolated, and everyone's laughing at you except Dad, who's really trying to help. Sounds to me like your unconscious wants you to give some thought to some of your new experiences lately, to look at them from your family's point of view (especially your dad's), and to take it all with a sense of humor.

on him with one of the other guys in the group.—‹‹daniela››

The One Where I Really, Really Wanna Strip!

I had a dream where I'd won some sort of contest. My "prize" for winning was to go up onstage and strip! You would think that I woulda been embarrassed and stuff, but I wasn't. I was happy to! When I got up onstage in front of the school, people started cheering. I started to strip and some guy told me I didn't have to end up completely naked. I was thinking, "But I want to!" Then I looked down the aisle and realized that it was being televised!!! But . . . I wasn't embarrassed. My dream ended once I was in my underwear.

—Ran77

★ ★ ★

Stand back, everybody. Ran77 is about to get a groove on. Naked!

Kidding. Getting naked in your dreams is all about exposing yourself. Not as in exposing your body, but as in exposing your inside self, your true col-

In my dream I was eating blue

ors. (Now's about the time you'd break into that awesome old Cyndi Lauper song, if you were into that.)

In this dream you need to show off your real self . . . not just onstage, but on TV for the whole world to see. In fact, it's such a cool idea for you that in your dream, it's a big ol' prize. You recognize how special it is to be able to be a true individual and not be afraid to show it off to other people.

Could that be because you feel there are people in your life (like the guy in your dream) who are constantly keeping you from being an individual? Or from letting everyone know who you really are inside?

You're one of a kind, Ran77. Just like everyone else. Let it out! (At least in your dreams!)

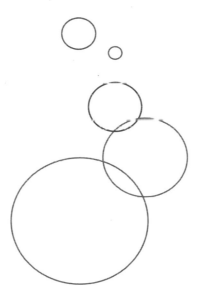

M&M's off my uncle's kitchen floor.—‹‹Jeannie››

The One Where My Grandma Makes Me Get Married

I dreamt I was getting married and my grandma, who died this summer, was planning it. I could tell she spent a ton of money on it, and everything was beautiful. As I started walking down the aisle in a heavily decorated chapel, I looked at the groom and I had no idea who he was! For some reason I was attracted to him but not in love with him.

Then I looked down at my dress, and to my horror, it was the ugliest turquoise, satin, eighties-style dress with huge puffed sleeves (yuck!). I started sobbing and screaming at my grandma for being such a control freak that she didn't let me pick out my own dress (isn't that mean?).

Then I ran outside where there were huge white tents with elaborate decorations and even maids and butlers setting tables! It was so beautiful! In the middle of the garden, there was an in-ground pool. I ran and jumped in with my dress on!

I hadn't noticed that the groom

I dreamed the sky turned orange-yellow

was running after me, and he jumped in the pool, too! He started begging me to come back, and then he started screaming and shaking me! And then I woke up. I would appreciate if you could explain this disturbing dream. Thank you sooo much!

—Disturbed

★ ★ ★

Don't panic. A wedding in your dreams represents a, well, wedding between you and a new idea or influence in your life. You're being connected with something, and there's a commitment involved.

The facts that you didn't plan this wedding, didn't know the groom, didn't even pick out your dress mean that somewhere you don't feel you're in control of these new influences.

Who's in charge? Grandma. Well, not really Grandma, but whatever it is that she represents to you. Hmmm. Old-school ideas? Tradition? Family?

But wait, there's more! You go plunging into a pool of water. Why? Well, water, in your dreams, is all about cleansing. You dive in there, trying to wash off this wedding, this new connection, including your dress. (It's interesting that your grandma picked your dress. Your clothes often represent how you present yourself to the world, and in your dream Grandma chose it. Frustrating!)

Anyway, there you are splashing around, and your groom jumps in with you! Could that mean you're not confident that you'll be able to wash off everything? That these ideas and influences will follow you even if you try and get rid of 'em? Uh, yeah. Probably.

Anyway, this is a dream to pay attention to. Who's defining you as a person? Make sure it's you.

after I fell off my skateboard.—‹‹LauraTaura››

The Ones Where I Cheat on My BF!

I always have dreams that I'm cheating on my BF, even though I really like him. Last night's dream was probably the worst out of all of them so far. I was at a hotel for the weekend with my best friends. Then all these popular guys came to our room, and I was totally flirting with one of them. This guy is usually really, really flirty and funny and everything, but this time he was acting like he really wanted to make out with me or something. (In real life I kinda like him, but I know that he doesn't like me.)

Anyway, we were getting really close, and just before we kissed, I woke up (what a terrible way to end a good dream!). I feel really guilty about these dreams. I like my BF a lot, and I don't really like this other guy that much. We are just friends who flirt (it's in both our natures, so it isn't anything new). What does this mean?　　　　　　　—Leeleen

★　　★　　　★

Don't freak, Leeleen. Everything's still cool in Leeleenland.

See, when you're all up in it with someone who's not your significant other, it means you're up for getting cozy with something that he represents to you.

So, what's he represent to you? Popularity? Probably, since that's how you described him. Making out with him is

I dreamed I saw this dairy cow getting ready to fall off a cliff.

about you getting a little closer to that popularity that he represents in your mind.

   Oh, and this dream doesn't mean things aren't going well with your boyfriend. In fact, it has nothing at all to do with your boyfriend. It has to do with your social situation and how you'd like to make some changes.

there's a big problem

with dream interpretation. See, it's really helpful
to talk about your dreams and to read books
and stuff to help you understand them, but in the
end, only you can really understand what you
dream about.

You heard it—you are the only one qualified
to interpret your dreams. And to top it off, most
dreams you analyze you'll never totally make
sense of.

But here's the thing: Going through the
process of interpreting your dreams is fun. Fun in
the same way looking through old pictures is
fun. Not fun like roller-coaster fun, but fun like
taking a personality quiz in a magazine. You
know what I mean.

And besides the fun part, analyzing your dreams will get you thinking about yourself and different parts of your life in all kinds of new ways. As in, finding out all kinds of new things about yourself.

It's up to you what your dreams mean, if anything. Taking a closer look at your dreams might reveal something amazing, or it might not. Listen to your instinct about whether or not it's really meaningful. Don't worry too much about the stuff that isn't. Remember: If you try hard enough, you can analyze the fun out of your dreams. Don't do it.

There's no foolproof method for understanding dreams, but there are techniques to get you close, which you'll find in this section. You need to break down your dream and take it step by step.

Your first task? Write down your dream as best as you can remember it. Oh, and use the present tense. You know, "I'm at a Tori Amos concert with my friends. Suddenly Tori turns into Michael Jackson and starts drinking a Snapple. . . ." Why present tense? So you can psych your brain into reliving the whole thing. You'll remember more details that way.

Once you've got it scribbled down, turn the page, and let's get started.

"OUR LIFE IS COMPOSED GREATLY FROM DREAMS, FROM THE UNCONSCIOUS, AND THEY MUST BE BROUGHT INTO CONNECTION WITH ACTION. THEY MUST BE WOVEN TOGETHER."
—ANAÏS NIN

Question 1: What Is the Mood of Your Dream?

Mood is important. Not your mood right now, but the mood of your dream. (Although I do care. How ya doin'? Good? Great. Let's move on.)

There's a good reason to answer this question first. Why? Because if you know the general mood of your dream, analyzing each of the bits and pieces with that in mind will be easier and will make more sense. For example, while you might assume that a dream about skeletons rising up from their graves in a cemetery would be a big, scary nightmare, if your overall perception of the mood in the dream is actually funny or hopeful or upbeat, you'd have to look for a different meaning in those skeletons.

★ *Alloy User Poll* ★

DO YOU DREAM IN COLOR?

80% Yeah! Full color!
4% Black and white, definitely
16% I'm not sure

When you answer this question, it should only be a word or two. Be precise. For example, "threatening" is better than "scary." "Relieved" is better than "happy." "It sucked" isn't as good as "It shocked." See? If you're not sure how to answer, come as close as you can. As you continue analyzing, you might think of a better way to describe in detail what you're really feeling.

Some things to think about:

How did you feel during the dream?

Formulate your feelings as

How did you feel when you woke up?

When you think about the dream, what emotions
do you feel?

Don't think too hard about this step. Listen to your
gut, let your instinct decide, and move on.

Some Examples of Mood

MY DREAM WAS . . .

✳ Hot and sexy	✳ Frightening	✳ Serene
✳ Tiring	✳ Boring	✳ Upbeat
✳ Frustrating!	✳ Otherworldly	✳ Funny
✳ Confusing	✳ Saddening	

OR MY DREAM MADE ME FEEL . . .

✳ Hopeful	✳ Dissed	✳ Ashamed
✳ Well treated	✳ Brilliant!	✳ Alive
✳ Hopeless	✳ Like I was	✳ Helpless
✳ Endangered	somebody else	
	✳ Exposed	

well as your thoughts.—A. R. Orage

Question 2: What Is the Setting of Your Dream?

Where your dream happens is mad important. That's why when people start talking about their dreams, they almost always start out, "I'm in . . . ," or, "I was in . . ."

Anyway, the setting usually tells you what part of your life or what part of yourself the dream is about. If it takes place in the house you lived in as a child, it may be a dream about something you've been dealing with for a long time. Or if it takes place in the middle of the ocean, it may be a dream about being isolated.

But here's the kicker: It's not so much about where it happens as about how the setting made you feel. That middle-of-the-ocean dream isn't necessarily a bad dream—that is, if you were psyched, not afraid, to be floating out there alone.

some common settings

- ★ In a house (Whose?)
- ★ In a big, open field
- ★ In a dungeon
- ★ At the movies
- ★ At the mall
- ★ On a staircase
- ★ At a concert
- ★ In the sky
- ★ At home
- ★ In a plane
- ★ In your car
- ★ At school
- ★ On a mountain
- ★ Underwater
- ★ In bed
- ★ In the shower
- ★ On a beach
- ★ On MTV

In dreams I never know where my mind is going to take me . . . partying

Some questions to help you think about setting:
* Do you recognize this place? Have you been there before?
* Do you feel safe there? Unsafe?
* Do you know where you are? Are you lost?
* Do you want to stay, or are you just passing through?
* Does the setting change during your dream? How does it change? Good to bad? Bad to good?
* Is it a twisted version of someplace you know from real life? If so, how is it different?

Pay Attention!

The weather in your dream has a big effect on the overall feeling and mood of your dream. (Unless your dream takes place indoors, that is, in which case there might not be much in the way of weather.) Here are a few weather conditions and what they might represent:

fair weather: *optimism*
thunderstorm: *conflict! change!*
cloudy weather: *confusion or uncertainty*
calm skies: *peace*
steady rain: *cleansing*
violent storms, tornadoes: *anger and/or helplessness*
cold front: *solitude*
heat wave: *sex*

on the coast of Hawaii or walking on the Great Wall of China. —‹‹Jamn››

⋆ By getting a clear picture of your dream's setting, you should start to get clues about what
the dream might be about and whether or not
it's a positive dream or, well, not. The most
important question: How did the setting make
you feel?

Question 3: Who Are the Characters in Your Dream?

**Every dream is full—of symbols, stories, emotions,
twists and turns, you name it. And it's all important
to your dream. But most of the time nothing sticks out
quite like the people.**

Sometimes friends show up. Or people in your family. Or

people you hate. Or characters from
TV shows. Or dead people. Or total
strangers. Or Brandy. Or Oscar de la
Hoya. Or Brandy and Oscar de la
Hoya. Or, well, pretty much anyone
could show up.

But it doesn't stop there. Characters
don't have to be people. They could be
animals, cars, computers,
or food. Aliens.
Ghosts. Marshmallow men.
Talking grapes. A banana
cream pie. Okay, what-
ever. But seriously,

Who would ever give up the reality of dreams for

anything in your dream that you interact with and that inter-acts with you pretty much qualifies as a character.

The most important character in your dream? Duh, you.

I know I've said it before, but I'm saying it again. I can't help it.

Every character in your dream is you, or part of you, or a personified version of something that's on your mind. Everything everyone does and says in your dreams is being controlled by your unconscious. It's your big ol' brain call-ing the shots.

This is really helpful when it comes to interpreting your dreams. Ask yourself how you feel about this person in real life or what qualities you associate with them. What do they represent to you? Do you admire them? Do they crack you up? Do you secretly kind of hate them?

Friends Acting Crazy!

Your best friend, who you love and trust more than anyone in the world, shows up in your dream and tries to murder you. What's up with that?

Well, breathe a sigh of relief. It's not really her. Or him. Or it. And no one's in danger.

Here's the deal: There's a personality trait or quality you see in them that your unconscious also recognizes in you, and it's got a conflict with another quality in your personality. Like, maybe that murdering best friend of yours represents your own tendency to pro-crastinate, which is showing up to get in the way of your success at school.

relative knowledge?—Alice James, <u>The Diary of Alice James</u>

Some common characters and what they often represent:
  * ★ Parents: authority, love, warmth, discipline
  * ★ Teachers: authority, learning, being tested
  * ★ Movie stars: glamour, excitement, freedom
  * ★ Friends: commitment, warmth, safety, trust
  * ★ Siblings: family, competition, rivalry

is this a dream? or is this the grammys?

So Brendan Fraser, Dolly Parton, Christina Ricci, and Elmo all showed up in your dream. What is this, another awards show?

Nope. It's not even really a dream about them. See, your unconscious, in your dreams, has a point to make. So it uses characters you'll recognize—familiar faces—to help make that point. In other words, Marilyn Manson made a guest appearance in your dream because he reminds your brain of something that it wants you to dream about.

Question 4: What Things Are in Your Dream?

Okay, time to make a list. Get out a piece of paper and pencil, or your laptop, or an Etch-A-Sketch. Or whatever.

Now, write down every single object or prop that you can remember from your dream. Every single one. The full moon.

The pay phone. A beagle. That bra. The set from *Who Wants to Be a Millionaire.* The Jennifer Aniston butter sculpture. The big black hole. If you can remember it, write it down.

Go back over your list, and next to each item write a sentence that begins, "It was as if . . ." (Hope you left some space next to each item.) For example:

The full moon—It was as if the moon was really important to me.

The pay phone—It was as if the pay phone was lonely—it had no wires, but it was brand-new.

The beagle—It was as if it was my dog (which I don't have in real life), and it was as if it was smarter, cleaner, and happier than I was.

✷ **Alloy User Poll** ✷

DO YOU APPEAR IN YOUR OWN DREAMS?

61% Always
38% Sometimes
1% Never

fragments / dropped from the day's caravan.—Rabindranath Tagore

Get the idea?

If you'd rather use something other than "It was as if . . . , well, see if I care. Use whatever you want. But make sure you write down more than what it looked like. Get in there how it made you feel and what impact it had on you in the dream. That's the important part.

Now, for each item write another sentence that begins, "Which reminds me of . . ." For this one think about what your sentence reminds you of, not the object.

★ Alloy User Poll ★

DO YOU EVER DREAM ABOUT CELEBRITIES?

19% Yeah, all the time!
67% Sometimes
14% Never, ever

For example:

The full moon—It was as if the moon was really important to me. Which reminds me of soccer practice.

The pay phone—It was as if the pay phone was lonely—it had no wires, but it was brand-new. Which reminds me of my friend Alec.

My beagle—It was as if it was my dog (which I don't have in real life), and it was as if it was smarter, cleaner, and happier than I was. It reminds me of my cousin.

Make sense? Obviously soccer practice doesn't look like the moon, but it's important to you. Alec doesn't look like a telephone pole (at least not exactly), but maybe he strikes you as a little lonely. And the beagle? Your cousin? Draw your own conclusions.

After you've finished, take a look at the whole list.

Why not go out on a limb?

Notice any themes? See any patterns? If you do sense a common thread to your dream, think about your real life. Anything going on that's similar?

Don't be too frustrated if you can't sense a pattern right away or if it doesn't remind you of anything right away. Just get your thoughts on paper and let 'em stew. Sometimes things don't make sense until later. Like when you're in the shower and all of a sudden you get it.

Dream Dictionaries

D *ream dictionaries aren't really all that.*

However, dream dictionaries can give you clues and even help you think about the things in your dream in a different way. They may bring you closer to the real deal. So if you must, look up stuff. Use more than one dictionary if you can. (There are plenty on-line, too.) Write the meaning given by the dictionary next to the words on your list. A dream dictionary, on the other hand, tells you what a symbol or an image might mean. Or even worse, what it means to the person who wrote the dictionary.

But do not do this step until you've completed your list and your "It was as if . . ." sentences. Repeat, do not. What you felt about the object is way more important than what it supposedly represents.

Isn't that where the fruit is? —Frank Scully

Question 5: What Is the Plot of Your Dream?

So, what happened in your dream?

Sure, the setting and the characters and everything are keys to understanding it, but what's even more important was what they did in your dream and how you reacted.

Think about it. If you have a dream about your brother, that's no big deal. But if you have a dream about your brother dressed up like Alanis Morissette and slicing up peeled bananas to decorate the garage, well, that's another story. And if your reaction in the dream is to think, Hey, great idea, and start growing bananas out of your ears and handing them over to him, then we've really got something juicy. (Yes, this is a real dream I recently had. I hope my brother doesn't read this.)

Often the most important action in a dream is to make a choice. In the above dream I made a choice not to be freaked out. In fact, I made a choice to pitch in. It says a lot about how I feel about my brother and the way he acts. It says even more about how I'd feel about my brother and the way he acts if he was a little crazier every now and then.

Choices are things like: Did I hide, or did I face up to that scary thing that's chasing me? Did I rescue the puppy or the baby? Did I go up the stairs to my bedroom where I'm comfortable or down the stairs to the basement that's really scary? Did I pick the flower or leave it alone?

Choices in your dream are important because they give you insight into yourself. Maybe it's a reflection of how you would act if you had to make a similar choice in real life—even a trial run for a decision you'll soon have to make.

Also consider how you felt about the choice. Was it predictable? Off the wall? Did things turn out the way you wanted them to? Did everything blow up in your face?

Remember that the action in your dreams doesn't have to be big and splashy to be noteworthy. Watching TV can be as significant as skydiving. What matters is how important it felt to you in the dream.

Warning! Warning! Warning!

Many times our dreams are about decisions we know we'll have to make in real life. Like where to go to college, or what haircut to get, or whether to turn in your druggie friend. You may not recognize the situation when you first look at your dream, but if you can place it, pay special attention to the outcome of your actions. If things turned out disastrously based on a choice you made, no matter how insignificant, your dream could be a warning from your unconscious to rethink things.

Question 6: How Does Your Dream End?

Sometimes the last impression you have of your dream tells pretty much the whole story. Kind of like how you can pretty much figure out an entire movie by watching the last few minutes.

But also like a movie, it's not just how the plot ended that matters. How did the characters end up? Did they change? What was the setting? Did it change? How about the mood? What was it at the end? Different than at the beginning?

was it really the end?

What we think is the end of the dream isn't always the end. See, even when we do remember our dreams, we often don't remember the whole thing. It's impossible to tell. Sometimes what we think is the end of our dream isn't really the end; it was simply the last or most important image we remember.

And most important, how did you feel at the end? Relieved? Happy? Terrified? Pissed off? Ecstatic? Exhausted? Anxious? Optimistic? Cautious?

Whatever you settle on to describe your dream, see how it meshes with your impressions from Question 5. Don't panic if they seem like they have nothing to do with each other, at least when you first look at them. Dreams have many layers and involve many emotions. Kinda like real life.

Question 7: What's the Title of Your Dream?

Episodes of *Friends* all have names that follow the same pattern: "The one where . . . ," and then they fill in the rest. "The one where Ross kisses the monkey" and "The one where Rachel sees Chandler nude and freaks out." It doesn't tell the whole, entire story, but it does tell the most significant or important thing that happened. The title also indicates what characters are involved and, if you're lucky, gives a sense of the mood.

So go ahead, give your dream a title. It should be no more than ten words (excluding "The one where . . .")

Some examples:

⋆ The one where I tried to save Claire Danes from a wolf

⋆ The one where I ran home after seeing I was nude

⋆ The one where Dad made me laugh by doing two Olympic-worthy tumbling runs

⋆ The one where I scored 1600 on my SATs, but I wasn't happy

⋆ The one where I tried to sell my sister

⋆ The one where I got attacked by a shark and panicked

In bed my real love had always been the sleep that

Get the idea?

Forcing yourself to reduce your dream to just a few words is a very good way of identifying what the dream was really about. Don't be satisfied with a title that doesn't feel like it covers the important stuff. If the title includes a choice you made, an outcome, a reaction, or a relationship, you're probably going in the right direction.

Don't worry if no one else would ever really understand it. Your title should work for you. As long as you get a mental picture of the dream—and how it felt—when you see the title, you're in good shape.

Your title will also help you remember your dreams in the long run, and if you keep a list of titles, you may even begin to see patterns. For example, if you write down fifteen dreams and seven of them have to do with you being nude, then you might want to take a closer look at those dreams, comparing and contrasting them using the seven questions. It'll be easier to figure out why your unconscious keeps going back to those themes.

rescued me by allowing me to dream.—Luigi Pirandello

Putting It Together

There. We've completed all the steps for understanding your dream. Would now be a good time to mention the fact that there is no such thing as a formula for understanding your dreams?

Okay, wait. Before you get all ticked off that you went through all these steps for nothing, relax. It wasn't for nothing. It's just that the payoff is subtler than you might have expected.

See, each step made you think about the dream in a different way, paying attention to different parts of it.

Thinking about the mood of your dream might tip you off to what emotions you have in your brain that might have contributed to this dream.

Looking at the setting helps you understand what part of your life or what part of your mind the dream is about.

Understanding the characters and images in your dream helps you think about yourself in terms of the people and things in your real life and how you feel about them.

Paying attention to what happened in your dream, especially what you did, should make you

Trust yourself. You know more

look at your real life and the choices you make there.

Knowing how your dream ended and how you felt about it at the end indicates whether there's a lesson in there and what that lesson is.

Finding a simple title for your dream helps you remember it easily so you can think about it again in the future. Looking at the same dream more than once can reveal more than one meaning or message.

So what we've done by breaking this sucker down and looking at its parts is relate it to all the different parts of your life, from your past to your present, from your unconscious to your conscious, from your fears to your hopes and wishes. And if we're lucky, all this breaking down gave you a clue. And if we're really, really lucky, it gave you a flash.

one more thing to think about . . .

If you had this dream again, what would you have done differently in it? Why? If it were your conscious self taking part in the same situation, what would you have done? Answering this question might help you figure out what your dream is trying to tell you or what about your personality it's trying to help you figure out.

than you think you do.—Dr. Benjamin Spock

The Flash

You know the feeling when something all of a sudden makes sense. Jung called it a "click." Some people feel like their stomach goes empty all of a sudden. Maybe it's a sudden zone out where all you can think is, Yeah! That's it! Maybe your knees buckle.

I call it "the flash."

What is it? Well, it's the moment when you realize something truly important. Somewhere, from your brain, from your unconscious, from your stomach, from outer space, from wherever, comes a heads up. "Yo! That's what this is about!"

No dream book can give it to you; no dictionary can serve it up. Not even a personal meeting with a dream therapist can take you to the flash. All these things can help. All these things can get you close. But only you can make the flash.

That is, if there is one. In my experience, the flash comes only sometimes. Not every dream analysis will result in a flash. And hey, that's all right. It's fun, anyway. And who knows? Answering the seven questions is like inputting all that information into your brain. Eventually maybe you'll figure it out—even if it's not in the front of your mind. You could have a flash many days after your evaluation. Or even have a dream with the flash in it.

It is only with the heart that one can see rightly.—Saint-Exupéry

The Seven Questions!

1. What is the mood of your dream?

★ ★ ★

2. What is the setting of your dream?

★ ★ ★

3. Who are the characters in
your dream?

★ ★ ★

4. What things are in your dream?

★ ★ ★

5. What is the plot of your dream?

★ ★ ★

6. How does your dream end?

★ ★ ★

7. What's the title of your dream?

★ ★ ★

Dream Catching: Journals, Drawings, and Friends

Yeah, okay, so the first thing you think of when someone tells you to put some effort into keeping track of your dreams is, "Great. More homework. Thanks a lot."

But don't freak. It's not all that hard. It doesn't take all that much time. And catching your dreams is absolutely the most important part of analyzing and understanding them.

Still sound like a pain in the neck? Don't worry, it's not. Here's why:

★Reason 1: Catching your dreams can actually be kinda fun.

★Reason 2: You'll have lots of material for that screenplay you'll write someday.

★Reason 3: You'll be really proud of yourself.

★Reason 4: Looking back on dreams you've caught will help you see patterns and help you understand what your unconscious is up to.

★And Reason 5: You can do it any way you want. There are many, many ways of

I have a dream catcher above my bed.

recording your dreams. It's not only about keeping a journal. You can write poetry, make pictures, role-play with your friends, and, oh yeah, you can keep a straight-up journal, too.

One very important thing to remember: Write down your dreams before you go about analyzing them. In fact, write 'em down before you've really had any chance to think about them. That way you'll be sure to record the dream, the whole dream, and nothing but the dream.

no more nightmares

Many Native Americans would hang "dream catchers" near their beds. Designed with a spider's web in mind, they were meant to capture dreams as they swirled around the dreamer. When the person woke up, the first thing they'd see was the dream catcher, which would help them remember any dreams they'd had. Some people also believe dream catchers intercept nightmares before they make it into your head.

KEEPING A JOURNAL

Keeping a dream journal is the most effective, precise, and complete way to make a record of your dreams. It's simple, it's cheap, it lasts, it's personal, and it's really not all that hard.

Of course, the idea of staring at a blank page first thing in the morning when all you really want is a couple of Pop-Tarts or a latte can be nauseating. But before you bug, read these tips. They'll help, I promise.

Check it out:

* No one else will read this journal but you. It doesn't have to be perfect. You can even mis-spell stuff and use poor grammar. Rite real bad if you wanna. Cuss all you want. Ha ha. No, seriously, the journal is for you, so don't worry about how it seems. As long as you understand it, that's all that matters. Oh, and no points off for bad penmanship.

* Don't make your dream logical unless it already is. Once you start trying to make your dream make sense as you write it down, you're try-ing to fit it into the real world. And dreams don't. That's the whole point. So let 'er rip. The weirder, the better. Remember, do not

The palest ink is better

start to analyze until you've finished writing it down.

★Don't try to fill in any blanks. Be sure to write down only what you remember. If there are gaps or blank spaces— like, say, how you got from the top of the Washington Monument to backstage at the David Letterman show, don't worry about them. If you try to fill them in, your dream won't be your dream anymore; it'll be something else.

★Focus on feelings, moods, emotions, stuff like that. It's not just who's in your dream and what happened that matters. How you felt in the dream is important. Yeah, you got lost crawling around there in Mariah Carey's extensions, but how did it make you feel?

★Use all kinds of memory. Close your eyes and visualize what happened. Block your ears and try to re-create the sounds you heard. Clear your mind and re-feel the feelings you had. It's not just how you ate that MP3 player for breakfast, but what it tasted like matters, too.

★Write down all your dreams, not just the ones that you think are important. That really stupid dream you had last night about not being

★ ★ ★ Alloy User Poll ★

DO YOU WRITE DOWN YOUR DREAMS?

20% Yeah, lots
53% Maybe once or twice
27% No way

than the best memory.—Chinese proverb

don't wait.

You gotta write your dreams down ASAP. That means in the middle of the night if you have to, in the dark. Or first thing in the morning, even before you pee. This is the hardest part about dream catching because it takes effort to get stuff down on paper in the middle of the night when all you want to do is turn over and crash. *(Always keep journal and pencil near your bed. Pencil, not pen . . . pens have a way of running out of ink in the middle of the night.)*

able to fit into your socks might actually have something useful in it.

* Use whatever you want for a journal. A $.99 spiral notebook works just as well as that $19.99 dream journal they stick in your face at the bookstore.
* Keep it short if you want to! Make it long if you want to! No grades.

So give it a shot. And be realistic. Just one dream at a time. No reason to promise yourself that you'll write down every single dream for the rest of your life. Just committing to writing down the next dream you remember will get you rolling.

"I WANT TO TURN MY DREAMS INTO SOMETHING TANGIBLE."

—CLAUDIA SCHIFFER, on how she's changing her life by keeping a dream diary next to her bed, to *In Style* magazine. Dudes, if she can do it, so can you.

If we cannot catch them as they are passing out at the

DREAM ART

Okay, so not everyone's a wordsmith. Some of us draw better than we write. Or at least we're able to communicate our feelings and impressions artistically, not verbally.

But don't start thinking that you can't catch your dreams if English isn't your best subject. There are plenty of ways for you to record your dreams. Like making drawings.

Maybe it looks like a cartoon, with a bunch of different scenes that recreate the dream. Or maybe it's more like a collage, with many drawings and things clipped from magazines to represent the parts of your dream. Maybe it's a quick sketch. Who knows? Whatever works for you.

Even if you're not a journal keeper, read pages 123 to 126 (journal section) because you'll want to keep in mind many of the same ideas. Like knowing that you don't have to show it to anyone if you don't want to. And paying atten- tion to the mood, not just the plot. And not getting tied down by logic. And doing it soon, like before your feet hit the floor.

Creating pictures or whatever to represent your dream takes more focus than writing it down. After all, you have to deal with the materials you're using, you have to have space to work, all that. Sometimes it's way smarter to jot down a few words or sentences that help solidify the vision of the dream in your head so you don't lose sight of your inspiration.

DREAM POEMS

Dreams are weird. They don't follow the same kind of logic that the real world supposedly does. Which sometimes

door, we never set eyes on them again.—William Hazlitt

makes them hard to write about. How can you put intelligent sentences together in proper English (or whatever language) if the stuff doesn't even make sense in the first place?

Write poetry, that's how.

See, just the way dreams are wacky and don't follow any rules, poems can be the same. You get to do whatever you want, write whatever comes to your mind, break all the rules—just like your dream did. Plus like poetry, dreams are often colored more by mood and emotion than by facts.

But before you start composing "Ode to My Weird Dreams," make sure you have all the tidbits you want to include nice and clear in your mind. That might mean writing down a bunch of key words to remind you what your dream was about. Or it might mean going through your magnetic poetry kit and pulling out all the pertinent words. Or whatever. But if you really want your poem to represent your dream, try to include all the important parts.

(If you want your poem to be, well, just a poem, that's awesome, too. Lots of writers and poets use dreams for inspiration.)

Firehouse
I waited
For the truck to round the corner
I hoped
For the heroes to arrive
I trusted
That they'd make it in time.
But my house burned anyway.
—LaritzaD

Airborne
Flying feels like falling,
Until you flap your wings.
I see the world underneath,
All trees and people and things.
I'm not sure where I'm headed,
But I seem to have a course.
This flying thing's way better
Than riding some dumb horse!
—Lilmil

birds.—Iris Murdoch, <u>The Sacred and Profane Love Machine</u>

Dream Buddies

One of the best ways to start remembering more dreams and understanding them is by talking about them a lot. Unfortunately, you can't just run around all the time gabbing in everyone's ear about what rap star showed up in your dream last night. Unless you live in some sort of dream-institute colony or something.

Solution? Get a dream buddy. Yep, a partner-in-dreams. A copilot for the journey through your dreamland. A co-captain of your dream team. Okay, yeah, you get the idea. Believe it or not, just by making a deal with a friend to help each other remember and understand dreams, you'll start remembering way more of them. Recount one scene out loud, and all of a sudden these other scenes come

back into your mind. These conversations usually include many versions of, "Oh yeah, then there was that other thing. . . ."

Make sure you and your dream buddy check in with each other every day to see if you've got anything to discuss. And you should get together around once a week in person to go through your dreams.

Infinite sharing is the law of

Stuff you can do together:

* Read to each other from your journals. Don't just hand over your journal. Make sure you read it aloud. Your buddy won't really understand the moods and emotions of your dreams unless you use your voice.

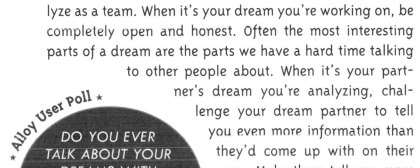

* Go through the seven questions together, and analyze as a team. When it's your dream you're working on, be completely open and honest. Often the most interesting parts of a dream are the parts we have a hard time talking to other people about. When it's your partner's dream you're analyzing, challenge your dream partner to tell you even more information than they'd come up with on their own. Make them tell you more details about the parts they think aren't all that important. Help them figure out what the people and things in their dreams are about—and offer lots of suggestions they haven't thought of yet. Do your best to think with an open mind, and try to find different points of view for your partner.

* Act out your dreams for each other. Believe it or not,

physically walking and talking your way through your dream will help you remember stuff you probably forgot. Some dream therapists believe there's no better way to remember stuff.

★Set up a 24/7 dream hot line. Your parents will love this one. Not. Got a phone in your room? Great. Let your dream buddy know the lines are open any old time he/she wants to discuss a dream—especially if they wake up in the middle of the night with an especially random one. (They can always leave a detailed voice mail if you just can't face a chatty friend.) Take it to another level by agreeing to call each other at like 4:30 in the morning a couple of times— when you're woken suddenly in the middle of the night, you remember your dreams better.

★Take notes and remember your buddy's dreams. Over time you might be able to see patterns that they haven't seen yet.

There's something about having a dream buddy counting on you that makes you more likely to remember your dreams. I guess it's the power of suggestion. . . . Tell yourself you've got to remember some dreams, and you will.

Put off thy cares with thy clothes; so shall thy rest strengthen

Sleep to Dream

Here's a no-brainer for you. The better you sleep, the better you dream. If you don't sleep well, your dreams suck, or, even worse, you won't remember them at all. It's that simple.

So here are the ten rules for a perfect night's dreaming:

1: Go to bed when you're sleepy!!

Being tired and being sleepy are two different things. Being tired can last all day. But being sleepy happens in waves that come around every hour to hour and a half. They last only five or ten minutes or so. Gotta catch 'em when they happen, or you'll have a much harder time falling asleep. Hint: Reading a few more pages or waiting to see the end of *The Late Later Latest Show* can screw you, making you miss your window of sleep opportunity. Don't do it.

2: Make sure you've had a full day, including some exercise.

You don't need to compete in an Ironman Triathlon before you sleep, but your body should be a little bit tired. Make sure that you've expended plenty of energy—mental and physical—so that you're actually looking forward to getting in bed at the end of the day. The more restful your sleep, the better your dreams.

3: Keep it dark and quiet.

Light is a major enemy of sleep. And therefore a major enemy of dreams. That's why human beings generally sleep at night and why they generally stay awake during the day. (Exceptions to this rule usually don't sleep all that well—ask 'em.) Do your best to make sure your bedroom is as dark as it can be and quiet, too. Loud noises really suck. If they're loud enough, they'll even worm their way into your dreams—like that annoying song that works its way uninvited into your dream because you left the stereo on.

TV is sleeping's worst enemy. And it's not at all helpful for dreaming, either. It's noisy and distracting, meaning you don't sleep as much or as deeply, and the images and sounds can take over your brain while you're asleep, bumping your own dreams to the back burner. (Note: Steady, quiet noises might actually help you sleep. . . . Some people like to have a fan or air conditioner on while they're sleeping. The low, quiet noise helps drown out other loud noises that get in the way.)

4: Get the temperature right.

Often when you wake up in the night and don't know exactly why, it's because the temp's not right. Temperature is one of those things where if you get it right, you don't even notice it. If you get it wrong, you're bumming. Me, I like it mad cold in my bedroom and mad warm under the covers.

5: Don't live the rest of your life in bed.

Bed is for sleeping. Okay, well, there are a few other things that are appropriate to do in bed. But doing homework, watching TV, eating meals, exercising—these aren't things that you should do in bed. Make your bed all about sleeping and dreaming.

Take rest; a field that has

6: Avoid big meals, especially ones with caffeine and sugar. But don't go to bed starving, either.

Contrary to popular belief, a wack meal won't give you wack dreams. But it could give you indigestion, or make you all gassy, or do other things that get in the way of restful sleep. On the other hand, having a totally empty stomach can interfere, also, making you wake up more often than you should and keeping you from REM sleep, the place where the best dreams happen. Coffee, chocolate, and caffeinated soda also get in the way of a good night's sleep way more than you think. Believe it or not, caffeine doesn't even peak for two full hours after you drink it. That means a 9:30 P.M. coffee won't even fully kick in until 11:30 and will stick with you much longer.

7: Stay on a schedule.

If you can, you should hit the sack at the same time every night. What with weekends and all, this might sound nearly impossible, but the more regular your schedule, the more likely you are to have a great sleep. Which means great dreams. Your body will get used to slipping into sleep every night at the same time and staying there for the same amount of time.

8: Don't lie around forever waiting to fall asleep.

If you can't sleep, get up and read for a bit. Or listen to some music. Or something. Preferably something boring that will help you get drowsy. See, the best way to keep yourself up all night is to lie there worrying, "I really wish I could fall asleep right now." And if you don't sleep well, you won't dream well. So if for whatever reason you're just not

rested gives a bountiful crop.—Ovid

clocking out, do something quiet, boring, and relaxing.

9: Dig your bed.

Bed should be one of those places you really want to be. So make it awesome! Get sheets that you really like (some people like flannel sheets, some people like linen sheets, some people like Batman sheets) and pillows that work for you. (Test them out at your local department store. They'll let you lay your head on them right there. I like soft, downy ones, but some people like hard ones.) Face it: You spend a third of your life in that bed. Dreaming. So make it rule.

10: Lay off the booze and butts and ixnay on the drugs.

Even though you might think that alcohol and sleeping pills make you sleep deeper, the fact is, they keep you out of all the best dream-producing sleep stages, including REM, which you really need to dream well. And nicotine, a stimulant, continues to rev your engines way after your last cigarette—which means your nerves are being worked way into the night, long after you've gone to sleep. Oh, and by the way, pot is a major problem—it totally screws your

feeling sleepy?

Teens and adults average about 7.5 hours of sleep a night. Regularly getting less than seven hours is considered unhealthy.

But lack of sleep isn't just annoying; it's dangerous. The U.S. Department of Transportation says falling asleep while driving causes more car accidents than anything else except drunk driving. As in, 200,000 accidents a year, resulting in 5,000 deaths. So let's all hit the sack.

But a man who doesn't dream is like a man who doesn't

short-term memory, so even if you do dream, you don't remember the dreams.

If all this chemistry doesn't work for you, try reading your chemistry textbook. That'll get you sleeping in no time.

★ ★ ★

"TOO SOFT A BED TENDS TO MAKE PEOPLE DREAM, WHICH IS UNHEALTHY AND WEAKENING."
——THE GIRL SCOUT MANUAL,
"HOW GIRLS CAN HELP THEIR COUNTRY" (PUBLISHED IN 1913)

★ Alloy User Poll ★

DO YOU GET ENOUGH SLEEP?
7% Yeah, more than enough
46% Just about right
17% Nope,
I need way more

★ ★ ★

"TO ACHIEVE THE IMPOSSIBLE DREAM, TRY GOING TO SLEEP."
——JOAN KLEMPNER

★ ★ ★

I THINK YOUR DREAM DEPENDS ON WHAT YOU HAD TO EAT THE NIGHT BEFORE . . . LIKE YA EAT CHEESE, YA GONNA DREAM ABOUT A RAT CHASING YOU DOWN A SEWER SYSTEM. IF YOU EAT SPACE STARS BEFORE YOU SLEEP, YOU ARE GONNA FALL OUT OF SPACE! IT'S A SIMPLE CONCEPT.
——TIFFAN

sweat. He stores up a lot of poison.—Truman Capote

★*Lavender.* A dab of lavender oil under your nose or on your pillow calms your brain. A low-burning lavender candle is cool, too, but make sure you blow it out before you fall asleep—or you could be living "The Burning Bed, Part Deux."

★*Chamomile.* A cup of hot chamomile herbal tea will soothe your nerves. Make sure it's steaming because breathing the vapor is just as important as drinking the tea. Chamomile dreams tend to be calmer than most.

★*Valerian root.* A drop of valerian solution or a couple of capsules helps you fall asleep a bit faster, but more important, it makes your night of sleep even more restful and dream filled than usual. Note: This stuff stinks like your older brother's feet, so brace yourself.

★*Mint.* A drop of peppermint oil on your temples or a cup of hot peppermint herbal tea kicks stress to the curb and can result in clearer, more vivid dreams. Take it even further with a small squeeze of lemon in your tea.

He only earns his freedom and

Top Ten Dream Themes

Hundreds of dreams are sent to us at Alloy every week. And lemme tell you, they are among the sickest, illest things I've ever read. But details aside, there are themes and elements in your dreams that come up more than any others.

(Okay, well, these are the top ten dream themes besides sex and death. Check out the deal on those on pages 18 to 19 and 36 to 37.)

1 FLYING

Flying dreams are by far my favorite. I've never had a dream where I soar up there like a hawk or anything, although I'd really like to, but I have dreams where I can do an extra-long long jump. Like, a twelve-block-long jump. I just pull up my knees and float along the street.

Some people's flying dreams have them sitting in a chair or steering their bike through the air E.T. style. No matter. It amounts to the same as flapping your arms—you're flying, and you're controlling it. (If you're flying in a plane or something, check out "Traveling" on page 143.)

Flying in your dreams is a shout out to freedom—either you wish you had more, or you're psyched about the freedom you do have. It's about new things happening in your life and seeing the world from a new perspective.

The thing about flying is, it depends on what else is going on in your dream, too. Like, flying to escape a situation is different from flying to show off. Flying to rescue someone is different from flying to get around an obstacle. Think about how you used flying in your dreams. Was it for fun? Was it to get away from something? Was it to get somewhere you felt you really needed to be?

Whatever the situation, think about what's similar in your real life. Are you wishing you had more freedom (like a later curfew) so that you could solve more problems (like hooking up)? Are you psyched about new freedom (like a car) and want to share it with others (like that hottie at the record store)? Are you desperate to get out of a situation (like an upcoming trig exam) and wish you had more freedom to get out of it (like a note)? Are you wishing you had more freedom to score a certain goal (like applying for that job)?

★ Alloy User Poll ★

DO YOU EVER DREAM ABOUT FLYING?

57% Yeah!
19% Nope
24% I'm not sure

When you've decided what your flying was about, figure out what adjustments you can make in your real life to increase or better use your freedom.

Lovers of air travel find it exhilarating to hang poised between

got pee?

If you dream about going to the bathroom, it's usually about getting rid of excess baggage. Unburdening yourself. Expressing ideas you're withholding.

Then again, have you ever had to pee really, really badly in your sleep and dreamed about trying to find a bathroom?

2. NUDITY

Everyone dreams about being nude in situations where it isn't all that cool to be nude. Like in the lunchroom. Or at Grandma and Grandpa's house. Or on *Jeopardy*.

What's it about? Well, being nude in your dream means you're revealing something about yourself that you're not used to showing off. Letting it all out, so to speak.

But it all depends on how you felt about being nudie-pudie. Were you totally cool with it? Then your dream was probably about feeling comfortable exposing something about yourself that you'd normally hide. Were you freaked? Then you're dreaming a straight-up insecurity dream.

Lots of times when I'm naked in my dream, no one else really seems to care. I'm all, "Where are my pants?" and they're all, "What time is it?" or whatever. What's that about? I think it's a dream to reassure me that revealing parts of myself might not freak people out after all. . . . In fact, they'll take it perfectly in stride.

Think about your nudity. How'd you feel about it? Were other people grossed out? Did you feel like you were in danger? Were you embarrassed? Proud? Cold?

the illusion of immortality and the fact of death.—Alexander Chase

3. FALLING

Falling dreams are so common that some people think they're throwbacks to our days as apes and monkeys.

Okay, that's cool. But there's also more to it. Falling signals a transition or change in the way you're approaching part of your life.

If you are up high and are falling toward the ground, you may be dealing with a problem from waaay up there in your head. So you fall back down, to earth, to figure out your answers from here.

If you're falling down into a hole, like Alice in Wonderland, you're falling into your unconscious, hopefully to find a solution to your real-world problems.

In other words, falling is like a huge signal to reevaluate how you're looking at your life or a part of it. Find a different point of view.

★ Alloy User Poll ★

DO YOU EVER DREAM ABOUT FALLING FROM A HIGH PLACE?

61% Yeah!
17% Nope
22% I'm not sure

4. SCHOOL

As if you don't spend enough time there, you also have to dream about it! Sucks, I know, but get used to it because people dream about school for their whole lives. See, being at school in your dreams means you're aware of a lesson you're learning in life.

Think about how you felt during your dream. Were you psyched to be in school? Or were you hating it? If you were psyched to be there, it probably means you've learned something lately that's made you a better person, or more confident, or closer to achieving a goal. If you were totally hating being at school, it probably means that you aren't feeling like you're doing so well in some of your life, like you're unprepared for some kind of test.

School dreams often have to do with situations you know you'll have to face in the near future. Whether or not you succeeded in your dream—as in, felt prepared, confident, and together—should tell you how prepared your unconscious thinks you are for the upcoming situation.

Check this: There's a difference between being "at school" and being "in the school building." If you're in the building in your dream but the action has nothing to do with schoolwork, then the building, if it's familiar (even if you've never been there in real life), is another version of your home. (See "Being in a House," on page 145.)

5. TRAVELING

Going somewhere in your dream? Driving? Riding? Walking? Standing on a moving sidewalk? Anytime you're going anywhere in your dream (but not running from a bad thing), your dream is about your journey through life.

Some important things to pay attention to: Are you in a car? Are you driving? Or is someone else? Did you decide to take this trip, or did someone else? If you're driving, you're feeling in control of the way your life is going. If someone else is driving, you're feeling like you aren't.

Cars, bikes, buses, motorcycles, airplanes, trains, whatever you're traveling in: These things represent your physical self, your body, the thing you use to travel through life. Is the car in good shape? Is it running well? Or is it in bad condition, or dented, or messed up? If it looks and feels good, you're feeling good about your physical state. If it doesn't, you're not.

How does the road ahead look? Bumpy? Or smooth? Are you late? Or right on time? Are you happy with the direction you're traveling in? Or are you about to drive off a cliff? If this journey feels good in your dream, you're probably psyched about the direction your life is taking and feeling good about your own "vehicle" and the direction it's heading. If not, pay attention to your direction and your relationship with your "vehicle" in your real life.

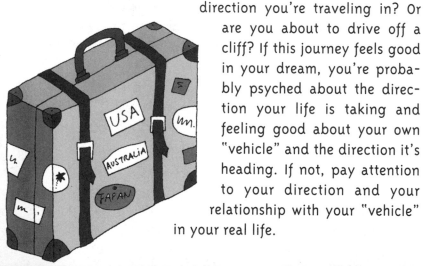

I dream I'm on an island with that foxy lady too, when I awaken,

6. BEING IN A HOUSE

Though not a theme exactly, houses appear in many of your dreams, and they can be pretty revealing. A house or building in your dream, especially one that feels familiar in some way, represents yourself.

It's normal to feel like you're at "home" in your dream, but you're actually in a house you wouldn't recognize in real life.

Each room (sort of) represents a different aspect of yourself.

Bathroom: There may be something in your life that you need to clean up or get rid of.

Kitchen: If there's not a lot of food in the kitchen, there may be something about your personality, or body, or mind that you need to feed. Better figure out what's hungry and what it needs. If there's plenty of food in your dream, you're feeling well nourished all over.

Living room: Focus on your relationships with people. Is the room chaotic? Maybe your social life is, too. Is the room empty? Maybe you're lonely or just peaceful and quiet. Do you feel happy in this room? You're happy with your friends. Is the room tense? Maybe there's a relationship you need to tend to.

Bedroom: This room can go a couple of directions, depending on what happens in your dream. It has to do with relaxation and peacefulness as well as sex. Pay attention to your state of mind in the dream. . . . If it is confident and happy, great. If it is confusing or bizarre or scary or generally bad, you might not be happy with those parts of your life.

I must have been mistaken, I'm on Third Avenue.—Beastie Boys

Upstairs: This part of the house represents what you want to be or do in life. Your aspirations, your goals. It also represents your spiritual side. If you're happy up there, you're happy with your goals, and your spirit is in good shape. If it's scary or gross or ugly up there, your spiritual side needs some attention.

Downstairs/basement: Downstairs represents your unconscious mind. Your instincts. Your urges. Your dark side or all that stuff you do that you feel you shouldn't be doing. It represents your fears, especially the ones you feel silly having. How you deal with the stuff in your basement indicates how much power your fears have over you in real life. Are they easy to handle? Tough?

7. PREGNANCY

Okay, I admit it. I've had lots of birth dreams in my life. I've given birth to babies. To furniture. To animals. Even to Meredith Baxter, who played the mother on *Family Ties* back in the eighties sometime. Go ahead, call me a freak.

But know this: Being pregnant or having a baby in your dream can happen to anyone—male or female. All it represents is something new or different in your life. Pay attention to how you feel about the baby. Are you happy about it? Are you freaked? Are you

You shoot me in a dream, you

afraid you can't deal? Are you disgusted? How you feel about whatever it is you gave birth to is how you feel about the new thing or idea or solution that is entering your real life.

8. VIOLENCE

Violence in dreams represents conflict between two (or three, or four, or many) parts of your brain or two ideas, or two opinions, or two somethings in your head. Lots of times the people or things duking it out or shooting it out or whatever (whether you're one of them or not) are people who you associate closely with the thoughts or ideas that are fighting. Like, if you're smacking your school principal across the face, your dream could be about your wish for freedom and the reality of discipline.

If something really awful happens to you in your dream, like you're attacked and injured, it could mean you're punishing yourself on some level for something you've done or thought in real life. When you attack someone in your dream, it means you're railing against whatever it is they represent to you. If you're totally winning your fight, like whaling on 'em, it means you're confident about an obstacle you're facing in life or faced before. And if you're stuck in a fight with someone but you just can't win, it could be all about feeling helpless somewhere in your life.

When something violent or bloody happens in my dreams, most of the time I pay attention, but I'm all, "Yeah, whatever," about it instead of being freaked out like I would be in real life. Lucky for me, that's normal.

better wake up and apologize.—Quentin Tarantino

See, my brain knows it's not real, so I watch it like I'd watch it on TV. I think about it, but I'm not horrified. Usually.

9. GETTING LOST

By now you've probably got a pretty good idea how to look at things in your dreams in new ways. Like, if you get lost in some forest or something in your dream, it doesn't mean you're going to be the next Hansel or Gretel. It means you're feeling some confusion about an aspect of your life. Your unconscious is unclear or uncomfortable with how you're dealing with the confusion, so out pops a dream about being lost.

Usually the confusion responsible for dreams like this is confusion about yourself. You being lost in your dream is kind of like you being lost somewhere in your brain. You're discovering or investigating unknown territory. Pay attention to what the place you're lost is like. Is it a really thick forest? Then you may be in a really crowded part of your brain with lots of different ideas and thoughts. A wide-open plain? You may be in a vast, lonely part of your brain you haven't paid all that much attention to yet. Is it stormy? You might have pressing issues in there. Sunny? Things might be in good shape. Were you lost in a place you felt like you should know really well? Then things in your head might be a little different from what you assume they are.

It's mad important to figure out how the whole experience of being lost made you feel. Were you scared? Excited?

If you think that you're strong enough,

Intrigued? Were you confident that you'd find your way? Was there hope?

This is a dream where the ending, if you can remember it, is superimportant. If you found your way, it means you have the confidence to deal with the real-life issue at hand. If you didn't, it means you aren't so sure.

10. FOOD AND EATING

It may not often be front and center in your dreams, but food is an element that plays a big role in them. Food in dreams is about all kinds of input. In other words, nourishment to all your parts: body, mind, soul.

Is there tons of yummy, delicious food? You're feeling well nourished. A little hungry in your dream? Then something's not getting the input it needs. Is the food in your dream really nasty? You might be feeling that some "input" you've been getting or giving yourself is bad. Ate too much? You might be smacking yourself for being too greedy somewhere in life. Was it a big, happy meal with people you love? Then maybe all the different parts of your brain are getting along. Are you eating something really unusual or chowing down someplace that seems really odd? Then you're getting or craving new ideas, new input.

Pay attention to how you felt about the food and what role it played. You'll figure it out.

Oh, and duh: There's a whole side to food that's mad sexual. You know, that whole putting-things-into-holes thing.

Dream Colors

"What color was my dream?" The question doesn't really make all that much sense, and neither will the answer, but ask yourself, anyway, and blurt out the first color that comes into your head. (Don't force it if nothing comes to mind.)

PINK: Love, plain and simple.

RED: Passion. Intense love or intense anger.

BLACK: Your unconscious mind. Also loneliness.

GRAY: Confusion, like being in a fog.

WHITE: Truth, especially a hidden truth being exposed. Also a new beginning.

GREEN: Nature. Growth. Problems being solved.

BLUE: Sometimes this means sadness or melancholy. But it also represents the sky, higher powers, spirituality.

YELLOW: Peacefulness and happiness . . . and sometimes authority.

it's personal

Our perceptions of colors and numbers are very personal and sometimes very different across cultures. The color yellow always makes me think of heat and warmth, but to someone with a Chinese background it may signify authority (Chinese tradition said that only the emperor was allowed to wear yellow). Check your own head—what comes to your mind when you think of certain numbers or colors?

Some things in my dreams are in vibrant

Dream Numbers

Sometimes numbers play important roles in your dream. Maybe it's dancing numerals like they have on <u>Sesame Street</u>, or sometimes there's just an overwhelming sense that there's a number associated with your dream. When you think of your dream, what's the first number that comes to mind?

I. Uniqueness. Being happy with yourself. A solo act. Or isolation and feeling lonely.

2. Balance. Symmetry. Love. Yin-yang. Father and mother.

3. Strength. Mind/body/spirit.

4. Stability. Four seasons. Four directions.

5. The human body. (Think about yourself spread-eagled—you have five points. One head, two arms, and two legs. See? Five.)

6. Divine love. Uh, okay.

7. Luck!

8. Completion. Picture the number itself—it's a totally enclosed, never-ending line.

9. Triple strength. As in, three times three.

10. Authority. Law. You know, like the Ten Commandments.

colors and others are in black and white.—‹‹Nashall››

The End

So there you have it. A little heads up on dreams and what they are, a few clues on what means what, some really weird dreams, and a tip or two on how to make your own dreams a little better. Not bad.

I hope you've been having fun with this book. Like I said up front, that's what it's all about.

I also hope this book helps you figure out that dreaming is a really cool part of life—not just something that happens on the side. The more you pay attention to your dreams, the more intense they'll become . . . and those eight hours you spend socked out will become some of the most exciting hours of your day.

Keep this book next to your bed so that the next time you wake up in a panic because a walrus with Hillary Clinton's voice stole your socks, you'll be able to remind yourself that it's just a dream—and read about dreams that are even more whacked than your own. Oh, and if you can't fall back asleep, you can always read the science part (pages 44 to 49) over and over again. That oughtta put you out.

Dream on.

To accomplish great things, we must dream. —Anatole France